Intro

ICON
International Communication Through English

Donald Freeman

Kathleen Graves

Linda Lee

Boston   Burr Ridge, IL   Dubuque, IA   Madison, WI   New York   San Francisco   St. Louis
Bangkok   Bogotá   Caracas   Kuala Lumpur   Lisbon   London   Madrid   Mexico City
Milan   Montreal   New Delhi   Santiago   Seoul   Singapore   Sydney   Taipei   Toronto

ICON International Communication through English, 1st Edition
International Edition 2005

Exclusive rights by McGraw-Hill Education (Asia), for manufacture and export. This book cannot be re-exported from the country to which it is sold by McGraw-Hill. The International Edition is not available in North America.

10 09 08 07 06 05 04 03 02 01
20 09 08 07 06 05 04
CTF   MPM

ICON Intro Components

Student Book
Workbook
Teacher's Manual
Audio Cassettes
Audio CDs

ICON Teaching-Learning Video

When ordering this title, use ISBN 007-124078-0

Printed in Singapore

Acknowledgments

The authors would like to thank the many people around the world who have provided invaluable feedback through reviewing and class testing ICON. In particular, we would like to thank:

Nely Barbosa Brock, Ana Carla Calabria, Roberto Soares Dias Junior, Julita Ribeiro Ferreira, Patricia Norma Gilardi, Itana de Almeida Lins, Juliana Valadares, **ACBEU,** Salvador, Brazil; Dr. Nicholas Dimmitt, **Asian Institute of Technology,** Thailand; Paul Humphries and Dee Parker, **AUA,** Bangkok, Thailand; Silvia Correa, Sonia Hobbs, Adriana Beneduzzi Passarelli, Jean Ewert Santos, Luiz Otavio de Barros Souza, Marilia de Moura Zanella, **Associação Alumni,** São Paulo, Brazil; Tsylla Balbino, Isabela Villas Boas, Marcella Ferreira Brotto, Carla Arena de Aquino, Maria da Luz Silva Delfino, Aldenir Brito de Sousa, Flavio Mariano, Rosangela Tiyoko Matsunaga, Ana Maria Pohl, Vania Rodgrigues, **Casa Thomas Jefferson,** Brasilia, Brazil; Yu-Chen Hsu, **Central University,** Taiwan; Shu-Fen Huang, **Chung Wen University,** Taiwan; Kathi Jordan, **Contra Costa College,** California; Shou-Shen Lu, **Cultural University,** Taiwan; Patrick Hwang, **E.Future,** Korea; Chi-Rei Ting, Li-Chi Yueh, **Fu Jen University,** Taiwan; Laura MacGregor, **Gakushkin University,** Tokyo, Japan; Greg Cossu, **Greg's English,** Takarazuka, Japan; Joe Luckett, Wilma Luth, **Hokusei Gakuen University,** Hokkaido, Japan; Michel Englebert, Rebecca Fletcher, Joo-Kyung Park, **Honam University,** Korea; Shi-Yun Huang, **Hsin Pu Technology Institute,** Taiwan; Sonia Bueno, Rosali Erlich, Monica Alcantara Marzullo, Doraliz Nogueira, Zaquia Lavi Tabach, **IBEU,** Rio de Janeiro, Brazil; David McMurray, **Kagoshima International University,** Japan; Robin Strickler, **Kansai Gaidai University,** Osaka, Japan; Alexis Kim, Korea; Louie Dragut, Michelle Kim, Kevin Price, Neal D. Williams, **Kyung Hee University,** Seoul, Korea; Kazuyoshi Sato, **Nagoya University of Foreign Studies,** Japan; Johanna Katchen, **National Tsing Hua University,** Hsinchu, Taiwan; Aaron Campbell, Barbara Stein, **Ryukoku University,** Japan; Susana Christie, **San Diego State University,** California; Sally Gearhart, **Santa Rosa Community College,** California; Dr. Won Moon Song, **Silla University,** Pusan, Korea; Tai-Yung Lee, Yu-Hwa Lee, **Soo Chow University,** Taipei, Taiwan; Fairlie Atkinson, Damian Benstead, Kevin McEwen, Ron Schafrik, Nathan Stewart, **Sungkyunkwan University,** Seoul, Korea; Kathleen Tice, Richard Tice, **Soonchunhyang University,** Korea; Shi-Tei Shai, **Taipei Business Institute,** Taiwan; Co-Chon Tsai, **Taipei Technology Institute, Taiwan;** Chung-Jei Tsen, **Taipei Technology Institute;** Ann-Marie Hadzima, **Taiwan National University,** Taipei; Lourdes Solis, **Technological Institute of Monterrey,** Mexico; Patricia Krejcik, Rosemarie A. Lemmerman, Aurea Camargo Ribeiro, Ligia Salgado Saad, **UCBEU, São Paulo,** Brazil; Dixie Santana, **Universidad Panamericana,** Guadalajara, Mexico; Morris Kimura, Hiromi Middleton, Tara O'Brien, **Vermont Adult Learning,** Vermont; Susan Dunlap, **West Contra Costa USD,** California.

We would also like to thank: Henry Hirschberg, Ed Stanford, Steve Van Thournout, Sam Costanzo, Tina Carver, Juanita Thompson, the exacting Nancy Jordan and the inimitable Thomas Healy at McGraw-Hill. Thanks also to Emily and Laura for their wise suggestions.

Contents

UNIT	LISTENING	LANGUAGE FOCUS	PRONUNCIATION
GETTING STARTED **Greetings and Introductions** page 2			
Unit 1 **Is Korean food spicy?** *Kinds of food* page 4	Conversation: *Is it expensive?*	Yes/no questions with *be*	Intonation of *yes/no* questions
Unit 2 **Where is volleyball popular?** *Describing sports* page 10	Global Interviews: *What sports are popular?*	Wh- questions *(what, where, why)* with *be*	Intonation of *wh-* questions
Unit 3 **The nightlife is great!** *Describing places* page 16	Conversation: *How's the weather?*	Pronouns *(It* and *They)*	Syllable stress in adjectives
REVIEW OF UNITS 1–3 page 22			
Unit 4 **It's terrific dance music.** *Kinds of music* page 24	Global Interviews: *What do you think of samba?*	Yes/no questions with *do* and *does*	Reduced form of *Do you*
Unit 5 **I don't like horror movies.** *Kinds of movies* page 30	Conversation: *Everybody likes action movies!*	Singular and plural forms	Word stress in sentences
Unit 6 **Do you like to eat out?** *Fun things to do* page 36	Conversation: *What do you want to do tonight?*	Questions with *like to, want to,* and *prefer to*	Reduced form of *want to*
REVIEW OF UNITS 4–6 page 42			

CONVERSATION STRATEGY	INFOZONE (Read/Speak/Write)	RECYCLING
Saying you don't know	**Reading:** Global Village Restaurant Menu **Write** about your favorite dish.	*What's your name?*
Asking for reasons	**Reading:** World Sports **Write** about a sport.	Yes/no questions with *be* Saying you don't know
Showing you are interested	**Reading:** Great Places to Visit **Write** about an interesting place.	*Wh-* questions with *be* Asking for reasons
Explaining your answers	**Reading:** Music and Dance Scene **Write** about an event.	*It/They + is/are + adjective* Saying you don't know
Pausing expressions	**Reading:** Movie Reviews **Write** about a movie.	*Do you like _____?* *Wh-* questions with *be*
Repeating to check understanding	**Reading:** Free Time Around the World **Write** about an activity you like to do.	Yes/no questions with *do* Adjectives: *boring, relaxing, cheap* Asking for reasons

UNIT	LISTENING	LANGUAGE FOCUS	PRONUNCIATION
Unit 7 **When do you have lunch?** *Daily routines* page 44	Global Interviews: *What's your daily routine?*	*Wh-* questions (*when, what*) with *do/does*	Reduced form of *wh-* questions
Unit 8 **I never get enough sleep!** *Healthy and unhealthy habits* page 50	Conversation: *You look great!*	*How often* + *do/does* Expressions of frequency (*every day,* etc.)	Word stress in sentences
Unit 9 **Did you go to the gym?** *Weekend activities* page 56	Conversation: *How was your weekend?*	Past tense	Past tense *–ed* endings
REVIEW OF UNITS 7–9 page 62			
Unit 10 **Is there an ATM around here?** *Directions, neighborhoods* page 64	Conversation: *Is there an easy way to get downtown?*	*Is there/are there* Prepositions of location	Initial *th* sounds
Unit 11 **I want to buy a CD.** *Things to buy* page 70	Global Interviews: *When do you give gifts?*	Count and non-count nouns	Plural *–s* and *–es* endings
Unit 12 **That's a nice jacket!** *Clothes* page 76	Conversation: *How was your trip?*	Present continuous	Reduced forms of *what are* and *what is he*
REVIEW OF UNITS 10–12 page 82			

Pronunciation   page 86
Vocabulary Summary   page 94
Irregular Verb Chart   page 100
Credits   page 101

Conversation Strategy	Infozone (Read/Speak/Write)	Recycling
Showing you are listening	**Reading:** Good Luck Routines **Write** about a good or bad luck routine.	Yes/no questions with *do* Showing you are interested
Asking follow-up questions	**Reading:** Living longer **Write** about a tip for living longer.	Yes/no questions with *do* *Want to* Wh- questions (*when, what*) with *do/does* Showing you are interested
Turning the conversation around	**Reading:** Weekend Goals and Accomplishments **Write** about your weekend.	Verbs: *get up, go, play, take* Showing you are interested
Asking for repetition	**Reading:** It's a Great Neighborhood! **Write** about your neighborhood.	Past tense *Want to* Asking follow-up questions
Making suggestions	**Reading:** Shopping from Home **Write** about your shopping habits.	Past tense Asking follow-up questions Showing you are interested
Expressing surprise	**Reading:** : School Uniforms **Write** about clothes you wore to school.	*How often + do* *Do you like to . . .* Past tense *Wh-* Questions with *be* and *do* Asking follow-up questions

To the Teacher

ICON is a four-level integrated skills series that takes students from beginning to intermediate level. *ICON Intro* is the beginning level of the series.

ICON grew out of an in-depth research project into the role of course books in effective teaching and learning. From this research the series has distilled a set of activity types that create effective learner interaction in the classroom. Each unit of *ICON Intro* is designed around these core activities which were identified and developed through work with teachers who routinely teach at this language level. The core activities provide a structure which scaffolds the students' language learning experience. The scaffolding is achieved in the following ways:

1. The activities are sequenced to build gradually and systematically from more tightly focused to more open-ended language learning interactions.

2. The activity types recur throughout the book, making it easier for teachers to initiate student interaction in the class, since the activities become familiar to students.

3. Many activities are color-coded blue and yellow which clearly shows students *'who does what'.*

4. The units have a consistent structure which supports students' confidence and independence.

5. The target language is recycled within and across each unit of the book.

This scaffolding makes *ICON* transparent and easy to use in both small and large classes.

COMPONENTS:

While the **Student Book** is the heart of the series, *ICON* has a concentric design; each component builds on and extends the others in an integrated, expanding system. The **Interleaved Teacher's Manual** gives detailed suggestions for how to use the Core Activities effectively, in addition to providing variations, expansion activities and culture notes. The **Teaching-Learning Video** (which is intended to be viewed by teachers and students) presents the Core Activities in short animated clips, clearly showing teachers and students alike how to participate in the *ICON* classroom. Through this integration of **Student Book**, **Teacher's Manual** and **Teaching-Learning Video**, the *ICON* series weaves together teaching and learning explicitly so that teachers and students can achieve their aims.

The following components are also available:

- The **Workbook** provides additional practice for students within or outside the classroom.

- The **Audio Program** (available as audio cassettes and audio CDs) contains recordings for all the listening activities in the Student Book. It features a variety of native English speakers in addition to some non-native voices and accents.

- The **Assessment Package** has placement, mid-course and final tests as well as comprehensive guidelines on how to assess oral communication.

ICON INTRO CORE ACTIVITIES

YOU FIRST introduces students to target language which they can use immediately.

PRONUNCIATION is practiced in the context of the target language.

In **PAIR UP and TALK**, and **REPORT**, students personalize learning by sharing their own preferences and experiences.

5 I don't like horror movies.

1 VOCABULARY: *Kinds of movies*

A. YOU FIRST. Complete the sentences with *love, like, don't like* or *hate*.

1. I _____ comedies.
2. I _____ animated movies.
3. I _____ dramas.
4. I _____ musicals.
5. I _____ science fiction movies.
6. I _____ horror movies.
7. I _____ Jackie Chan movies.
8. I _____ action movies.

B. PRONUNCIATION. Listen and practice the questions you hear.

C. PAIR UP and TALK. Ask and answer questions about movies.

Do you like _____?
comedies   science fiction movies
animated movies   horror movies
dramas   Jackie Chan movies
musicals   action movies

Yes, I do.

Yes, I love them.

No, I don't.

No, I hate them.

D. REPORT. Tell your classmates one thing about you and your partner.

My partner and I both like _____ and _____.

30   UNIT 5   *I don't like horror movies.*

2 LISTENING: *Everybody likes action movies!*

A. LOOK/THINK/GUESS. Where are these people? Is Nick happy?

B. MODEL CONVERSATION. Listen and practice.

Clerk: Do you need some help?
Nick: Yes, can you recommend a good comedy?
Clerk: A comedy? Hmmm. Let me think. What about *The Power Game*?
Nick: *The Power Game*? Is that a comedy?
Clerk: Well no, it isn't. It's an action movie; but it's really great!
Nick: I don't like action movies.
Clerk: But everybody likes action movies. They're terrific.
Nick: Not me. They're not my thing.

IDIOM
They're not my thing. = I don't like them.

C. ACTIVE LISTENING. Listen to two more conversations. Check (✓) the answers.

	Conversation 1	Conversation 2
1. Who is the customer?	☐ man ☐ woman ☐ child	☐ man ☐ woman ☐ child
2. What kind of movie does the customer want?	☐ drama ☐ comedy ☐ science fiction movie	☐ action movie ☐ comedy ☐ musical
3. What kind of movie does the clerk recommend?	☐ Jackie Chan movie ☐ horror movie ☐ action movie	☐ animated movie ☐ horror movie ☐ Jackie Chan

UNIT 5   *I don't like horror movies.*   31

Activities are color-coded blue and yellow to make student interaction easier in large classes.

LISTENING activities introduce language in common situations. In addition, there are **GLOBAL INTERVIEWS** that present voices and opinions of people from around the world.

FOCUS ON IDIOMS highlights the English language as we really use it.

LANGUAGE FOCUS highlights language patterns and grammar points that serve communication.

MORE PRONUNCIATION PRACTICE provides additional pronunciation practice at the back of the book.

CONVERSATION STRATEGIES introduce students to simple but effective ways to manage and sustain conversations.

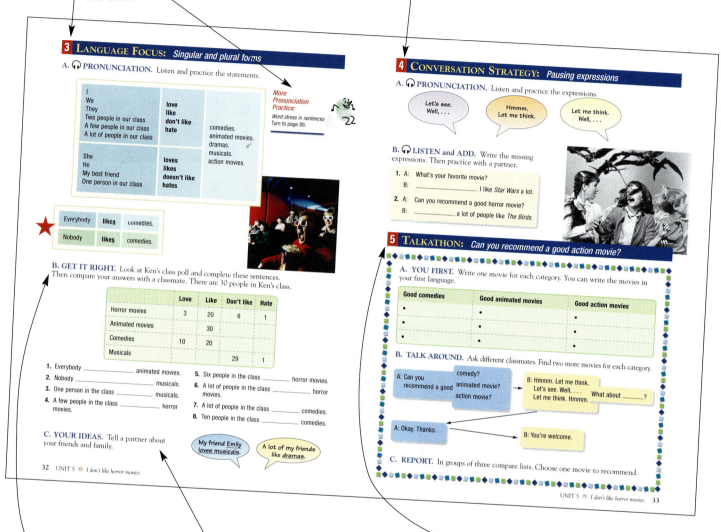

3 LANGUAGE FOCUS: *Singular and plural forms*

A. ⌂ PRONUNCIATION. Listen and practice the statements.

I We They Two people in our class A few people in our class A lot of people in our class	love like don't like hate	comedies. animated movies. dramas. musicals. action movies.
She He My best friend One person in our class	loves likes doesn't like hates	

More Pronunciation Practice:
Word stress in sentences
Turn to page 88.

Everybody	likes	comedies.
Nobody	likes	comedies.

B. GET IT RIGHT. Look at Ken's class poll and complete these sentences. Then compare your answers with a classmate. There are 30 people in Ken's class.

	Love	Like	Don't like	Hate
Horror movies	3	20	6	1
Animated movies		30		
Comedies	10	20		
Musicals			29	1

1. Everybody _____ animated movies.
2. Nobody _____ musicals.
3. One person in the class _____ musicals.
4. A few people in the class _____ horror movies.
5. Six people in the class _____ horror movies.
6. A lot of people in the class _____ horror movies.
7. A lot of people in the class _____ comedies.
8. Ten people in the class _____ comedies.

C. YOUR IDEAS. Tell a partner about your friends and family.

My friend Emily loves musicals.

A lot of my friends like dramas.

32   UNIT 5 ⌂ *I don't like horror movies.*

4 CONVERSATION STRATEGY: *Pausing expressions*

A. ⌂ PRONUNCIATION. Listen and practice the expressions.

Let's see. Well, . . .

Hmmm. Let me think.

Let me think. Well, . . .

B. ⌂ LISTEN and ADD. Write the missing expressions. Then practice with a partner.

1. A: What's your favorite movie?
   B: _____. I like *Star Wars* a lot.

2. A: Can you recommend a good horror movie?
   B: _____, a lot of people like *The Birds*.

5 TALKATHON: *Can you recommend a good action movie?*

A. YOU FIRST. Write *one* movie for each category. You can write the movies in your first language.

Good comedies	Good animated movies	Good action movies
•	•	•
•	•	•
•	•	•

B. TALK AROUND. Ask different classmates. Find two more movies for each category.

A: Can you recommend a good comedy? animated movie? action movie?

B: Hmmm. Let me think. Let's see. Well, . . . Let me think. Hmmm. What about _____?

A: Okay. Thanks.

B: You're welcome.

C. REPORT. In groups of three compare lists. Choose one movie to recommend.

UNIT 5 ⌂ *I don't like horror movies.*   33

GET IT RIGHT focuses on language accuracy.

YOUR IDEAS encourages students to talk about their own opinions and experiences.

TALKATHONS, ROLE PLAYS and **CONVERSATION MAPS** get students to activate vocabulary, language patterns and conversation strategies in fun, communicative ways.

The **INFOZONE** presents information in an appealing magazine format, encouraging students to read, write and talk about the topic.

READ ABOUT IT, **TALK ABOUT IT** and **WRITE ABOUT IT** provide a step-by-step approach to reading and writing.

READ ABOUT IT helps students to understand the reading text and graphics.

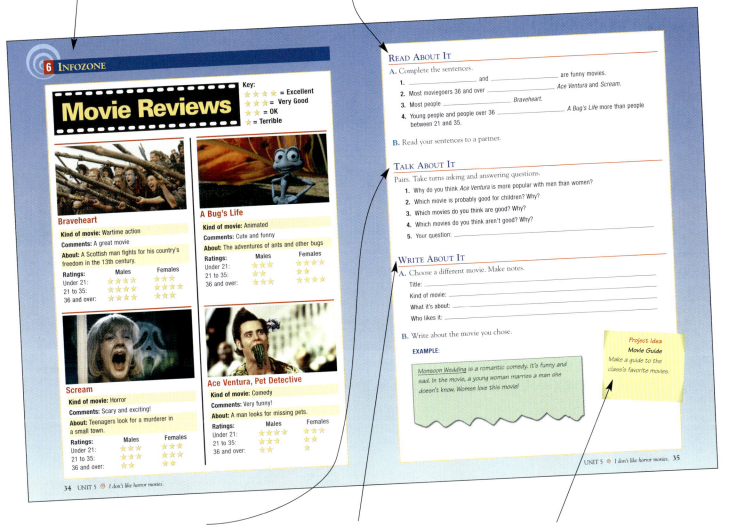

TALK ABOUT IT leads students to make inferences about the reading and to share opinions about the topic

WRITE ABOUT IT has a prewriting stage to help students develop their ideas.

PROJECT IDEA allows for expansion of the topic presented in the unit.

OTHER FEATURES OF *ICON INTRO*

Getting Started This is a short unit focusing on the language of introductions. It can be used as an icebreaker and as a way for the class to get to know each other.

Review Units There are four review units (after Units 3, 6, 9 and 12) which help students review and consolidate what they have learned through pair work and information gap activities.

Getting Started

1 NICE TO MEET YOU

A. 🎧 **PRONUNCIATION.** Listen and practice.

> Hi, I'm Silvia Santos.

> Hi, my name is Ken Park.

> Nice to meet you, Ken.

> Nice to meet you, too.

B. TALK AROUND. Introduce yourself to five classmates.

2 HOW DO YOU SPELL . . . ?

A. 🎧 **MODEL CONVERSATION.** Listen and practice.

Woman:	What's your name?
Mimi:	Mimi Koh.
Woman:	How do you spell your first name?
Mimi:	M-I-M-I.
Woman:	How do you spell your last name?
Mimi:	K-O-H.
Woman:	K-O-H?
Mimi:	That's right.

B. 🎧 **ACTIVE LISTENING.** Listen to the conversations. Circle the correct spelling.

1. a) Jane Reaves
   b) Jane Reeves

2. a) Zeke Quincy
   b) Zeke Quincey

3. a) Cindy Jeong
   b) Cindie Jeong

4. a) Walt Hukawa
   b) Walt Fukawa

5. a) Mabel Huxley
   b) Mable Huxley

5. a) Rita Mendes
   b) Rita Mendez

3 WHAT'S YOUR NAME?

A. TALK AROUND. Interview 3 classmates. Write their names in the chart.

EXAMPLE:
A: What's your name?
B: James Bond.
A: How do you spell your first name?
B: J-A-M-E-S.
A: How do you spell your last name?
B: B-O-N-D.

First name (Given name)	Last Name (Family Name)
James	Bond
1. _____	_____
2. _____	_____
3. _____	_____

4 INFORMAL GREETINGS

A. 🎧 PRONUNCIATION. Listen and practice.

1.
Ken: Hi, Silvia.
Silvia: Hi, Ken.
Ken: How's it going?
Silvia: Great!

2.
Mimi: Hi, James.
James: Hi, Mimi.
Mimi: How're things?
James: Not bad!

B. TALK AROUND. Greet five classmates.

How's it going?   Great!   How're things?   Not bad!

1 Is Korean food spicy?

1 VOCABULARY: *Kinds of food*

A. YOU FIRST. What are your favorite kinds of food? Check (✓) two kinds.

1. ☐ Italian food   **2.** ☐ Indian food   **3.** ☐ Korean food

4. ☐ Japanese food   **5.** ☐ Chinese food   **6.** ☐ French food

B. 🎧 **PRONUNCIATION.** Listen and practice the kinds of food above.

C. PAIR UP and TALK. Interview a partner.

What's your name?

My name is _____.

What are your favorite kinds of food?

_____ and _____ food.

D. REPORT. Tell your classmates about your partner.

My partner's favorite kinds of food are _____ and _____.

A. LOOK/THINK/GUESS. What kinds of restaurants are in the picture?

B. 🎧 **MODEL CONVERSATION.**
Listen and practice.

Nick: Let's have Indian food. The Bombay Palace is good.

Gabby: Is Indian food spicy?

Nick: Yes, it is.

Gabby: I don't like spicy food.

Nick: Well, how about that French restaurant?

Gabby: No way! It's too expensive.

> **IDIOM**
>
> **No way** = NO!

C. 🎧 **ACTIVE LISTENING.** Listen to the rest of the conversation. Check (✓) the restaurant Nick and Gabby choose.

☐ Bombay Palace ☐ Cafe Paris

☐ The Global Village ☐ The Milano

A. 🎧 **PRONUNCIATION.** Listen and practice the questions and answers.

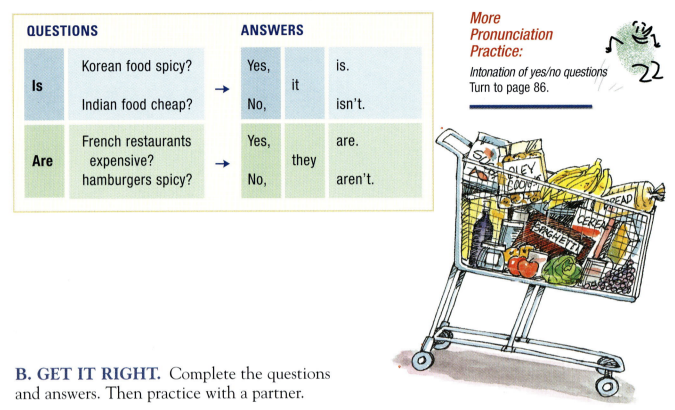

QUESTIONS		ANSWERS		
Is	Korean food spicy? Indian food cheap?	Yes, No,	it	is. isn't.
Are	French restaurants expensive? hamburgers spicy?	Yes, No,	they	are. aren't.

More Pronunciation Practice:

Intonation of yes/no questions
Turn to page 86.

22

B. GET IT RIGHT. Complete the questions and answers. Then practice with a partner.

1. A: _____*Is*_____ sushi Japanese?
   B: *Yes, it is.* _____

2. A: _____ bananas cheap?
   B: _____

3. A: _____ French bread good?
   B: _____

4. A: _____ Indian food your favorite kind of food?
   B: _____

5. A: _____ spaghetti Italian?
   B: _____

6. A: _____ cookies good for you?
   B: _____

7. A: _____ Italian food spicy?
   B: _____

8. A: _____ Chinese restaurants expensive?
   B: _____

C. YOUR IDEAS. Write more questions about food. Ask a partner your questions.

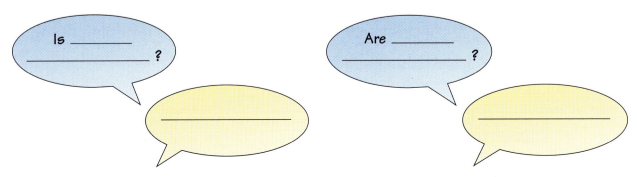

Is _____
_____?

Are _____
_____?

A.  **PRONUNCIATION.** Listen and practice the expressions.

I don't know the words in English.

I don't know.

I'm not sure.

Beats me.

B. 🎧 **LISTEN and ADD.**   Write the missing expressions. Then practice with a partner.

1. A: What's fondue?

B: _____

_____

2. A: What are crepes?

B: _____

_____

3. A: What's in feijoada?

B: _____

_____

4. A: What's a good French dish?

B: _____

_____

PAIR UP and TALK.   Take turns asking about different kinds of food.

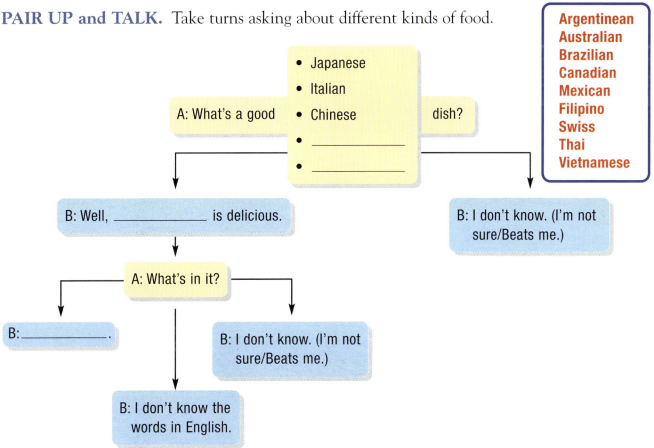

A: What's a good

- Japanese
- Italian
- Chinese
- _____
- _____

dish?

Argentinean
Australian
Brazilian
Canadian
Mexican
Filipino
Swiss
Thai
Vietnamese

B: Well, _____ is delicious.

B: I don't know. (I'm not sure/Beats me.)

A: What's in it?

B: _____.

B: I don't know. (I'm not sure/Beats me.)

B: I don't know the words in English.

Global Village Restaurant

LUNCH MENU

Indian

Vegetable Curry **$11.95**
Ingredients: Vegetables and spices
[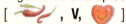 , **V,** 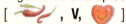]

Chinese

Kung Pao Chicken **$9.75**
Ingredients: Chicken, vegetables, spices [ ]

French

Crepes **$9.75**
Ingredients: Pancakes, cream, mushrooms [**V**]

Italian

Lasagna **$12.50**
Ingredients: Pasta, meat sauce, tomato sauce
and cheese

Japanese

Sushi **$15.25**
Ingredients: Fish and rice []

Korean

Bulgogi **$18.95**
Ingredients: Beef with vegetables

 = Spicy dishes   **V** = Vegetarian dishes (no meat)   = Low-fat dishes

READ ABOUT IT

A. Read the menu. Complete the sentences with *spicy*, *vegetarian*, or *low fat*.

1. Vegetable curry and Kung Pao chicken are _____ dishes.
2. Vegetable curry and sushi are _____ dishes.
3. Crepes and vegetable curry are _____ dishes.
4. Sushi and lasagna aren't _____ dishes.

B. Read your sentences to a partner.

TALK ABOUT IT

Pairs. Take turns asking and answering questions.

1. Which dishes on the menu are new to you?
2. Which dishes on the menu are *not* new to you?
3. Which is your favorite dish on the menu?
4. What are some other spicy dishes you know?
5. Your question: _____

WRITE ABOUT IT

A. Think of your favorite dish. Make notes.

Name of dish: _____

Nationality: _____

Ingredients: _____

B. Write about your favorite dish.

EXAMPLE:

> My favorite dish is bi bim bap. The ingredients are rice, vegetables, and a spicy sauce. It's a Korean food and it's delicious. Try it!

Project Idea
Menu: Class favorites
Design a menu with one favorite dish from each class member.

2 Where is volleyball popular?

1 VOCABULARY: *Describing sports*

A. YOU FIRST. *Do you think* _____*?* Check (✔) yes or no.

1. soccer is <u>fun</u>?
☐ yes ☐ no

2. golf is <u>relaxing</u>?
☐ yes ☐ no

3. basketball is <u>exciting</u>?
☐ yes ☐ no

4. skiing is <u>expensive</u>?
☐ yes ☐ no

5. auto racing is <u>dangerous</u>?
☐ yes ☐ no

6. baseball is <u>boring</u>?
☐ yes ☐ no

7. volleyball is <u>easy</u>?
☐ yes ☐ no

8. surfing is <u>difficult</u>?
☐ yes ☐ no

B. 🎧 **PRONUNCIATION.** Listen and practice the questions above.

C. PAIR UP and TALK. Ask and answer questions about sports.

| Do you think | golf soccer skiing volleyball surfing auto racing baseball basketball | is | fun relaxing exciting expensive dangerous boring easy difficult | ? |

Yes, I do.

No, I don't.

I don't know.

D. REPORT. Tell your classmates one thing about your partner.

My partner thinks _____.

A. 🎧 **FIRST LISTENING.** What sports are popular in each country? Check (✓) the answers.

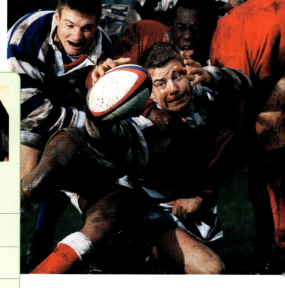

	Nelson *Brazil*	Amelia *The United States*	Paul *Australia*	Yasue *Japan*
soccer				
baseball				
basketball				
volleyball				
rugby				
surfing				

> **IDIOM**
>
> **be crazy about** = love

B. 🎧 **SECOND LISTENING.** Complete the statements.

1. *Nelson:* A lot of my friends play

   _____.

2. *Amelia:* I think _____

   is boring.

3. *Paul:* Australians are crazy about

   _____.

4. *Yasue:* _____

   is really a global sport.

C. PAIR UP and TALK. Where are these sports popular? Ask about each sport.

A: Where is <u>soccer</u> popular?

　　　baseball　　basketball

　　　volleyball　　rugby

　　　surfing　　_____

B: In _____ and in _____.

　Brazil　　the United States

　Australia　Japan

3 LANGUAGE FOCUS: Wh- questions with "be"

A. 🎧 **PRONUNCIATION.** Listen and practice the questions and answers.

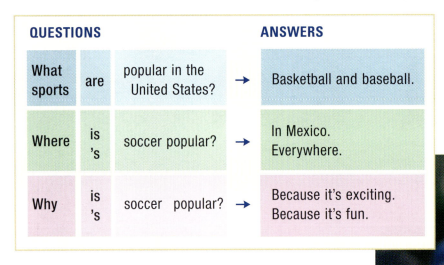

QUESTIONS				ANSWERS
What sports	are	popular in the United States?	→	Basketball and baseball.
Where	is 's	soccer popular?	→	In Mexico. Everywhere.
Why	is 's	soccer popular?	→	Because it's exciting. Because it's fun.

More Pronunciation Practice:

Intonation of "wh" questions Turn to page 86.

B. GET IT RIGHT. Complete the questions and answers. Practice with a partner.

1. A: What sports _____ popular in Brazil?
   B: _____

2. A: _____ is basketball popular?
   B: In _____

3. A: What sports _____ dangerous?
   B: _____

4. A: _____ sports are expensive?
   B: _____

5. A: _____ 's surfing popular?
   B: In _____ and Hawaii.

6. A: _____ 's golf popular?
   B: Because _____

7. A: _____ 's baseball popular?
   B: _____ Japan and _____

8. A: Where _____ soccer and skiing popular?
   B: _____

9. A: Why _____ auto racing popular?
   B: _____

10. A: Why _____ basketball popular?
    B: _____

C. YOUR IDEAS. Write more questions about sports. Ask a partner your questions.

What sports _____
_____?
_____

Where _____
_____?
_____

Why _____
_____?
_____

CONVERSATION STRATEGY: *Asking follow-up questions*

A. 🎧 **PRONUNCIATION.** Listen and practice the questions.

> *Why is that?*

> *Why basketball?*

> *How come?*

B. 🎧 **LISTEN and ADD.** Write the missing follow-up questions. Then practice with a partner.

1. A: What sports are popular at your school?

B: Hmmm. Volleyball and soccer are popular.

A: _____

B: Because our teams are great!

2. A: Is skiing popular too?

B: No, it isn't.

A: Really?

_____

B: Because it's expensive and dangerous.

3. A: What's your favorite sport?

B: Baseball.

A: Really?

_____

B: Because it's fun.

5 TALKATHON: *What's your favorite sport?*

A. YOU FIRST. Complete the sentences below.

> My favorite sport is _____.
>
> I think it's _____.

B. TALK AROUND. Talk to three classmates. Write their names and answers in the chart.

Name	What's your favorite sport?	Why is that?

C. REPORT. Tell about a classmate's favorite sport.

World Sports

U.S. snowboarder Kelly Clark, of Vermont, wins Olympic gold medal

Yao Ming, Chinese basketball superstar

▲ **Name of sport:** snowboarding
Kind of sport: individual
Equipment: snowboard, helmet
Who does it: snowboarders

▲ **Name of sport:** basketball
Kind of sport: team
Equipment: ball, hoop
Who does it: basketball players

◄ **Name of sport:** gymnastics
Kind of sport: individual
Equipment: bar, rings
Who does it: gymnasts

In many countries, children start gymnastics when they are young.

▼ **Name of sport:** taekwondo
Kind of sport: individual
Equipment: none
Who does it: taekwondo masters and students

▼ **Name of sport:** ice hockey
Kind of sport: team
Equipment: skates, helmet, puck, stick
Who does it: hockey players

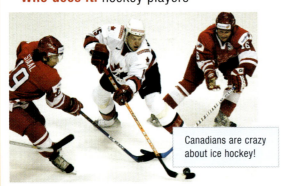

Canadians are crazy about ice hockey!

About 50 million people around the world practice taekwondo.

READ ABOUT IT

A. Complete the sentences.

1. _____ , _____ and _____ are individual sports.

2. _____ and _____ are team sports.

3. _____ and _____ use helmets.

4. _____ players use a ball.

5. I think _____ is exciting and dangerous.

B. Read your sentences to a partner.

TALK ABOUT IT

Pairs. Take turns asking and answering questions.

1. Which sports are new to you?

2. Which sports do you like to play?

3. Which sports do you like to watch?

4. What are some other team sports?

5. Your question: _____

WRITE ABOUT IT

A. Choose a sport. Make notes.

Name of sport: _____

Kind of sport: _____

Equipment: _____

Your opinion: _____

B. Write about the sport.

EXAMPLE:

Rugby is a team sport. Rugby players use a ball and goalposts. I think rugby is an exciting and dangerous game.

Project Idea
Culture Guide: Popular Sports
Make a guide for visitors about sports in your country.

3 The nightlife is great!

1 VOCABULARY: *Describing places*

A. YOU FIRST. Look at the pictures. Check (✓) your answers.

1. The weather is
   ☐ great ☐ terrible.

2. The shopping is
   ☐ wonderful ☐ terrible.

3. The nightlife is
   ☐ great ☐ awful.

4. The food is really
   ☐ good ☐ bad.

5. The public transportation is
   ☐ fantastic ☐ awful.

6. The traffic is
   ☐ OK ☐ horrible.

B. 🎧 PRONUNCIATION. Listen and practice the sentences above.

C. PAIR UP and TALK. Ask and answer questions about **your** city.

> What do you think of the _____?
>
> weather   traffic
> nightlife   shopping
> food   public transportation

> I think it's _____.
>
> ☺   😐   ☹
>
> wonderful   OK   terrible
> great   awful
> really good   horrible

D. REPORT. Tell your classmates one thing about your partner.

> My partner thinks the _____ here is great.

A. LOOK/THINK/GUESS. Where is Nick?

B. 🎧 **MODEL CONVERSATION.** Listen and practice.

Nick: Hello?

Gabby: Hello, Nick? It's Gabby.

Nick: Oh, hi Gabby.

Gabby: Where are you?

Nick: I'm in Miami.

Gabby: Wow! How are things there?

Nick: Not bad.

Gabby: Well, how's the weather?

Nick: The weather? Oh, it's fine.

Gabby: Oh yeah? That's good.

IDIOM

Not bad = OK

C. 🎧 **ACTIVE LISTENING.** Listen to the rest of the conversation. Complete the sentences.

1. The restaurants are _____.

2. The shopping is _____.

3. The nightlife is _____.

A. 🎧 **PRONUNCIATION.** Listen and practice the questions and answers.

QUESTIONS				ANSWERS		
How	is	the weather?	→	**It**	's	wonderful.
	's	the food?				
How	are	the stores?	→	**They**	're	great.
	're	the beaches?				

More Pronunciation Practice:

Syllable stress in adjectives
Turn to page 87.

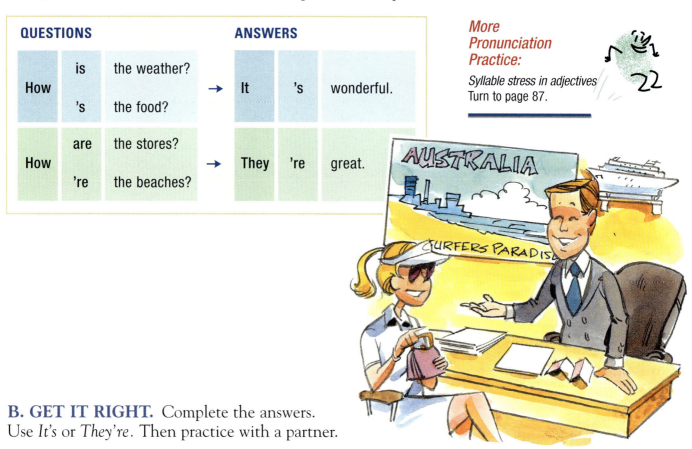

B. GET IT RIGHT. Complete the answers.
Use *It's* or *They're*. Then practice with a partner.

1. Customer: How's the weather in Australia?
   Travel agent: The weather? _____ great.

2. Customer: How are the restaurants?
   Travel agent: _____ really good.

3. Customer: Great. How are the nightclubs?
   Travel agent: _____ wonderful.

4. Customer: What about the skiing?
   Travel agent: _____ terrible — but the surfing is fantastic.

5. Customer: Really? How're the beaches?
   Travel agent: Oh, _____ beautiful.

6. Customer: How's the public transportation?
   Travel agent: Oh, _____ very good.

7. Customer: What about the traffic in Sydney?
   Travel agent: _____ not bad.

8. Customer: How are the museums?
   Travel agent: _____ OK.

C. YOUR IDEAS. Ask about your partner's favorite city.

What's your favorite city?

_____
_____

How _____ in _____?

_____
_____

4 CONVERSATION STRATEGY: *Showing you are interested*

A. 🎧 **PRONUNCIATION.** Listen and practice the expressions.

> Really?

> Oh, yeah?

> That's interesting!

B. 🎧 **LISTEN and ADD.** Write the missing expressions. Practice with a partner.

1. A: What do you think of New York?

B: Well, I think the people are really nice.

A: _____
How's the weather?

B: The weather? It's awful.

2. A: How are the restaurants there?

B: They're great.

A: _____
What's your favorite kind of food?

B: Chinese food.

3. A: How's the traffic in New York?

B: The traffic? It's awful.

A: _____
How's the nightlife?

B: Oh, it's wonderful.

5 TALKATHON: *Where's a good place for a vacation?*

A. YOU FIRST. Complete this sentence.

> I think _____ is a good place for a vacation because _____.
> *(name of a town or city)*

B. TALK AROUND. Talk to three classmates. Write their names and answers in the chart. Remember to show you are interested.

Name	Where's a good place for vacation?	Why?

C. REPORT. Tell about one of your classmates.

Great Places to Visit

▼ **Place:** Corcovado National Park
Country: Costa Rica
Why it's great: Beautiful beaches; great weather; lots of birds
Best time to visit: December to April

▲ **Place:** Santa Barbara, California
Country: U.S.A.
Why it's great: Great beaches; good surfing; good shopping; fantastic restaurants; international film festival
Best time to visit: March to November

▶ **Place:** Venice
Country: Italy
Why it's great: Fantastic restaurants; no traffic; great public transportation; beautiful city
Best time to visit: February to June, September and October

▲ **Place:** Natadola Beach
Country: Fiji
Why it's great: Beautiful white-sand beaches; good surfing and horseback riding; wonderful food; great weather
Best time to visit: May to October

◀ **Place:** Busan
Country: Korea
Why it's great: International film festival; fantastic restaurants; great shopping
Best time to visit: September to November

READ ABOUT IT

A. Complete the sentences.

1. There are great beaches in _____, _____ and
_____ .

2. The public transportation in _____ is great.

3. Santa Barbara and Busan both have an _____ .

4. Natadola Beach is good for _____ and _____ .

5. There are lots of great birds to see in _____ .

B. Read your sentences to a partner.

TALK ABOUT IT

Pairs. Take turns asking and answering questions.

1. Why is Venice a great place to visit?

2. Which place is interesting to you? Why?

3. Which place is *not* interesting to you? Why?

4. What are some other popular places to visit?

5. Your question: _____

WRITE ABOUT IT

A. Choose a place. Make notes.

Place: _____

Country: _____

Why it's great: _____

Best time to visit: _____

B. Write about the place.

EXAMPLE:

Veracruz is on the coast of Mexico. It's a fun city with great nightlife and terrific music. The restaurants are also good, and the shopping is not bad. The weather is usually sunny, and there's a nice beach nearby. Veracruz has a few interesting sights, such as an old fort and an aquarium. I think the best time to go is during Carnaval!

Project Idea
Map: Best Vacation Places
Draw a map with the best vacation places in your country.

Review of Units 1-3

1 CONVERSATION

A. Complete the conversation.

A: Hi, my _____ _____ Eva.

B: Hi, Eva. _____ Paulo.

A: _____ to meet you, Paulo.
Where _____ you from?

B: I'm _____ Brazil.

A: Really? That's _____ favorite place.

B: Oh yeah? Why is _____?

A: Well, the _____ is great.

B: Oh, _____ your favorite Brazilian dish?

A: _____ not sure. _____'re all delicious.

B. 🎧 Listen to check your answers. Then practice with a partner.

2 INFORMATION GAP

Student A, look at the information below. Student B, turn to page 84.

STUDENT A: Interview your partner and complete the chart.

A: Where's a good place to visit?

B: _____

A: What sports . . .?

B: _____

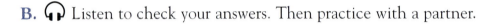

	Good place to visit "Where's a good . . ."	Popular sports "What sports..."	Popular foods "What kind of food..."	Weather "How's..."	Shopping "How's..."	Nightlife "How's..."
Student A	New York	🏀 ⚾	🍝	☹	☺	☺
Student B						

Play the two tic-tac-toe games with a partner. One person is X and one person is O. Take turns. Choose a square and complete the sentence. If it is correct, write your letter in the box. When you have three correct answers in a line, say "Tic tac toe!"

GAME 1

_____ is a good place to visit because _____ . ☐	Two expensive restaurants in my city are _____ and _____ . ☐	_____ is a vegetarian dish. ☐
The nightlife in my city is _____ . ☐	The weather is _____ today. ☐	_____ and _____ are dangerous sports. ☐
Unscramble: crazy/am/I/ about/sports ☐	*How come?* means _____ . ☐	Ice hockey is popular in _____ . ☐

GAME 2

Another way to say "I don't know." is _____ . ☐	_____ and _____ are outdoor activities. ☐	The best time to visit my country is _____ because _____ . ☐
_____ and _____ are cheap dishes. ☐	Unscramble: basketball/ popular?/is/ why ☐	_____ and _____ are popular sports in my country. ☐
Unscramble: Indian/spicy/is/ food. ☐	_____ is a boring sport. ☐	*Be crazy about* means _____ . ☐

4 It's terrific dance music.

1 VOCABULARY: *Kinds of music*

A. YOU FIRST. *Do you like _____?* Check (✔) *yes* or *no.*

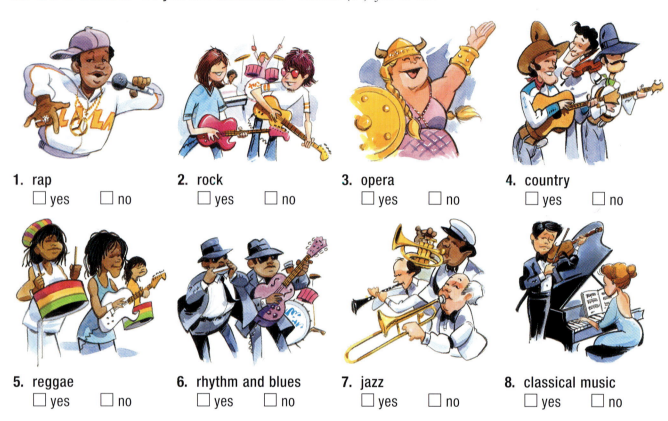

1. rap
   ☐ yes ☐ no

2. rock
   ☐ yes ☐ no

3. opera
   ☐ yes ☐ no

4. country
   ☐ yes ☐ no

5. reggae
   ☐ yes ☐ no

6. rhythm and blues
   ☐ yes ☐ no

7. jazz
   ☐ yes ☐ no

8. classical music
   ☐ yes ☐ no

B. 🎧 PRONUNCIATION. Listen and practice the questions above.

C. PAIR UP and TALK. Ask and answer questions about music.

Do you like _____?

rap	reggae
rock	rhythm and blues
opera	jazz
country music	classical music

Yes, I like it a lot.

It's okay.

No, I don't really like it.

D. REPORT. Tell your classmates one thing about your partner.

My partner likes _____ a lot.

A. 🎧 **FIRST LISTENING.** What kind of music does the person talk about? Match.

KIND OF MUSIC

1. Silvia
   Brazil

2. Donovan
   Jamaica

3. Steven
   The United States

bluegrass

ragtime

samba

salsa

reggae

B. 🎧 **SECOND LISTENING.** Write the kind of music next to each comment.

Comments	Kind of music
1. "I love it. It has a great beat."	_____
2. "It's really cool."	_____
3. "It's terrific dance music."	_____
4. "I don't like it."	_____
5. "It's different."	_____

> **IDIOM**
>
> **It's really cool.** =
> It's great.

C. PAIR UP and TALK. *What do you think of _____?*
Ask about each kind of music.

> A: **What do you think of _____?**
>
> bluegrass   reggae
>
> samba   _____

> B: _____.
>
> It has a great beat.   It's really cool.
>
> It's terrific dance music.   I like it a lot.
>
> I'm not familiar with it.   It's different.

A. 🎧 **PRONUNCIATION.** Listen and practice the questions and answers.

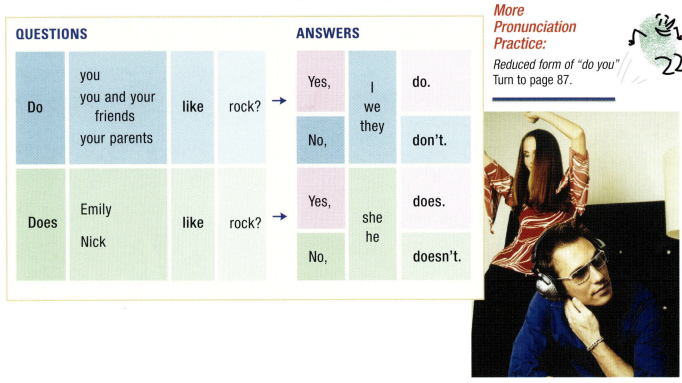

More Pronunciation Practice:
Reduced form of "do you"
Turn to page 87.

B. GET IT RIGHT. Complete the questions and answers. Practice with a partner.

1. A: _____ your friends like rock music?
   B: Yes, they _____

2. A: _____ your girlfriend like jazz?
   B: No, she _____

3. A: _____ you like classical music?
   B: No, I _____

4. A: _____ you and your friends like rhythm and blues?
   B: Yes, _____ _____

5. A: Does your teacher_____ reggae?
   B: Yes, _____ _____

6. A: _____ your parents like rock?
   B: Yes, they _____

7. A: _____ you and your brother like rap?
   B: No, we _____

8. A: _____ Rosa like opera?
   B: Yes, _____ _____

C. YOUR IDEAS. Write more questions about music. Ask a partner your questions.

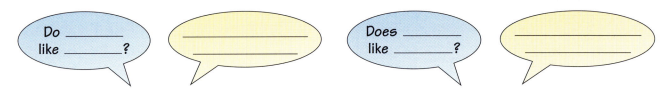

Do _____ like _____?

_____ _____

Does _____ like _____?

_____ _____

4 CONVERSATION STRATEGY: *Explaining your answers*

A. 🎧 **MODEL CONVERSATIONS.** Listen and practice.

1. A: Do you like Tori Amos?

B: Yes, I do. I think she's great.

A: Do you like Missy Elliot?

B: No, I don't. I don't like rap.

2. A: Do you like The Rolling Stones?

B: No, I don't. They're old.

A: Do you like The Dave Matthews Band?

B: Oh, yes. They're terrific.

B. FINISH IT. Complete the conversations. Then practice with a partner.

1. A: Do you like The Beatles?

B: _____, I_____. _____

2. A: Do you like Norah Jones?

B: _____, I_____. _____

5 CONVERSATION MAP: *Do you like the Happy Rappers?*

A. YOU FIRST. List your favorite musicians.

My favorite male singers are:	My favorite female singers are:	My favorite music groups are:

B. PAIR UP and TALK. Interview a partner about the musicians on your list.

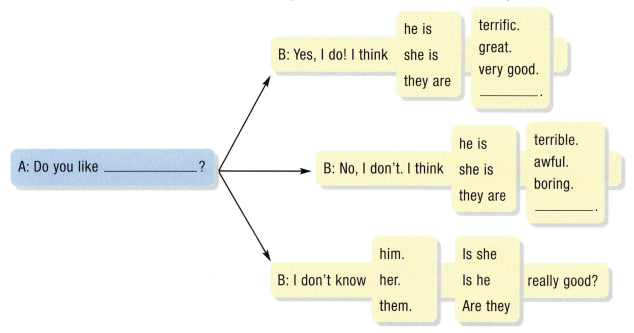

B: Yes, I do! I think | he is / she is / they are | terrific. / great. / very good. / _____.

A: Do you like _____?

B: No, I don't. I think | he is / she is / they are | terrible. / awful. / boring. / _____.

B: I don't know | him. / her. / them. | Is she / Is he / Are they | really good?

Weekend Scene

Music and Dance Scene

5/11–5/13

CHUCK'S BAR AND GRILL The one and only **Jim and His Cowboys!** They play great country music! 9 P.M. Friday

MEL'S PLACE This Saturday come and dance to the **Jamaican Wailers** from Kingston, Jamaica. Reggae with a great beat!

THE ALCAZAR
Fridays and Saturdays are Flamenco music nights. Dine and watch **Jorge and Pilar.** $50.00 for dinner and show.

THE APOLLO THEATER
May 12 and 13
Jo Marsfield's
Jazz Delight
Tickets $40–$150
"SOLD OUT"

THE LIVING ROOM This Saturday party with **Rocking Out.**
Entrance: Free
9:00–Midnight

READ ABOUT IT

A. Complete the sentences with kinds of music.

1. *Jim and His Cowboys* play _____ music.
2. *Jo Marsfield's* dancers dance to _____ .
3. *Rocking Out's* music is _____ music.
4. *Jorge* and *Pilar* dance to _____ music.
5. *Jamaican Wailers* play _____ .
6. On Friday you can listen to _____ music and _____ music.

B. Read your sentences to a partner.

TALK ABOUT IT

Pairs. Take turns asking and answering questions.

1. Why is the Alcazar expensive?
2. Which events are interesting to you? Why?
3. Which events are *not* interesting to you? Why?
4. What kinds of music do you like to dance to?
5. Your question: _____

WRITE ABOUT IT

A. Choose an event from page 28 or an event in your city. Make notes.

Name of place: _____

Name of band or dancers: _____

Kind of music or dance: _____

B. Write about the event you chose.

EXAMPLE:

Jorge and Pilar are at The Alcazar this weekend. They are Flamenco musicians and dancers. I like Flamenco music and dance. It's exciting and beautiful.

> **Project Idea**
> **Bulletin Board: Weekend Scene**
> Make a bulletin board with information about the weekend scene in your area.

5 | I don't like horror movies.

1 VOCABULARY: *Kinds of movies*

A. YOU FIRST. Complete the sentences with *love*, *like*, *don't like* or *hate*.

1. I _____ comedies.

2. I _____ animated movies.

3. I _____ dramas.

4. I _____ musicals.

5. I _____ science fiction movies.

6. I _____ horror movies.

7. I _____ Jackie Chan movies.

8. I _____ action movies.

B. 🎧 **PRONUNCIATION.** Listen and practice the questions you hear.

C. PAIR UP and TALK. Ask and answer questions about movies.

> Do you like _____ ?
> comedies   science fiction movies
> animated movies   horror movies
> dramas   Jackie Chan movies
> musicals   action movies

> Yes, I do.

> Yes, I love them.

> No, I don't.

> No, I hate them.

D. REPORT. Tell your classmates one thing about you and your partner.

> My partner and I both like _____ and _____.

A. LOOK/THINK/GUESS. Where are these people? Is Nick happy?

B. 🎧 **MODEL CONVERSATION.** Listen and practice.

Clerk: Do you need some help?

Nick: Yes, can you recommend a good comedy?

Clerk: A comedy? Hmmm. Let me think. What about *The Power Game?*

Nick: *The Power Game?* Is that a comedy?

Clerk: Well no, it isn't. It's an action movie; but it's really great!

Nick: I don't like action movies.

Clerk: But everybody likes action movies. They're terrific.

Nick: Not me. They're not my thing.

> **IDIOM**
>
> **They're not my thing.** =
> I don't like them.

C. 🎧 **ACTIVE LISTENING.** Listen to two more conversations. Check (✓) the answers.

	Conversation 1	Conversation 2
1. Who is the customer?	☐ man ☐ woman ☐ child	☐ man ☐ woman ☐ child
2. What kind of movie does the customer want?	☐ drama ☐ comedy ☐ science fiction movie	☐ action movie ☐ comedy ☐ musical
3. What kind of movie does the clerk recommend?	☐ Jackie Chan movie ☐ horror movie ☐ action movie	☐ animated movie ☐ horror movie ☐ Jackie Chan movie

A. PRONUNCIATION. Listen and practice the statements.

| I
We
They
Two people in our class
A few people in our class
A lot of people in our class | **love**
like
don't like
hate | comedies.
animated movies.
dramas.
musicals.
action movies. |
| She
He
My best friend
One person in our class | **loves**
likes
doesn't like
hates | |

More Pronunciation Practice:
Word stress in sentences Turn to page 88.

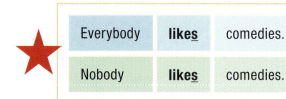

| Everybody | **likes** | comedies. |
| Nobody | **likes** | comedies. |

B. GET IT RIGHT. Look at Ken's class poll and complete these sentences. Then compare your answers with a classmate. There are 30 people in Ken's class.

	Love	Like	Don't like	Hate
Horror movies	3	20	6	1
Animated movies		30		
Comedies	10	20		
Musicals			29	1

1. Everybody _____ animated movies.

2. Nobody _____ musicals.

3. One person in the class _____ musicals.

4. A few people in the class _____ horror movies.

5. Six people in the class _____ horror movies.

6. A lot of people in the class _____ horror movies.

7. A lot of people in the class _____ comedies.

8. Ten people in the class _____ comedies.

C. YOUR IDEAS. Tell a partner about your friends and family.

My friend Emily loves musicals.

A lot of my friends like dramas.

A. 🎧 **PRONUNCIATION.** Listen and practice the expressions.

> Let's see.
> Well, . . .

> Hmmm.
> Let me think.

> Let me think.
> Well, . . .

B. 🎧 **LISTEN and ADD.** Write the missing expressions. Then practice with a partner.

1. A: What's your favorite movie?

   B: _____. I like *Star Wars* a lot.

2. A: Can you recommend a good horror movie?

   B: _____, a lot of people like *The Birds*.

5 TALKATHON: *Can you recommend a good action movie?*

A. YOU FIRST. Write *one* movie for each category. You can write the movies in your first language.

Good comedies	Good animated movies	Good action movies
•	•	•
•	•	•
•	•	•

B. TALK AROUND. Ask different classmates. Find two more movies for each category.

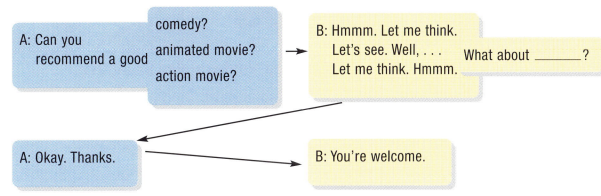

A: Can you recommend a good | comedy? / animated movie? / action movie?

B: Hmmm. Let me think. Let's see. Well, . . . Let me think. Hmmm. What about _____?

A: Okay. Thanks.

B: You're welcome.

C. REPORT. In groups of three compare lists. Choose one movie to recommend.

Movie Reviews

Key:

★ ★ ★ ★ = Excellent
★ ★ ★ = Very Good
★ ★ = OK
★ = Terrible

Braveheart

Kind of movie: Wartime action

Comments: A great movie

About: A Scottish man fights for his country's freedom in the 13th century.

Ratings:	Males	Females
Under 21:	★ ★ ★ ★	★ ★ ★
21 to 35:	★ ★ ★ ★	★ ★ ★ ★ ★
36 and over:	★ ★ ★ ★	★ ★ ★

A Bug's Life

Kind of movie: Animated

Comments: Cute and funny

About: The adventures of ants and other bugs

Ratings:	Males	Females
Under 21:	★ ★ ★	★ ★ ★ ★
21 to 35:	★ ★	★ ★
36 and over:	★ ★ ★	★ ★ ★ ★

Scream

Kind of movie: Horror

Comments: Scary and exciting!

About: Teenagers look for a murderer in a small town.

Ratings:	Males	Females
Under 21:	★ ★ ★	★ ★ ★
21 to 35:	★ ★ ★	★ ★ ★
36 and over:	★ ★	★ ★

Ace Ventura, Pet Detective

Kind of movie: Comedy

Comments: Very funny!

About: A man looks for missing pets.

Ratings:	Males	Females
Under 21:	★ ★ ★ ★	★ ★ ★
21 to 35:	★ ★ ★	★ ★
36 and over:	★ ★	★

READ ABOUT IT

A. Complete the sentences.

1. _____ and _____ are funny movies.

2. Most moviegoers 36 and over _____ *Ace Ventura* and *Scream*.

3. Most people _____ *Braveheart*.

4. Young people and people over 36 _____ *A Bug's Life* more than people between 21 and 35.

B. Read your sentences to a partner.

TALK ABOUT IT

Pairs. Take turns asking and answering questions.

1. Why do you think *Ace Ventura* is more popular with men than women?

2. Which movie is probably good for children? Why?

3. Which movies do you think are good? Why?

4. Which movies do you think aren't good? Why?

5. Your question: _____

WRITE ABOUT IT

A. Choose a different movie. Make notes.

Title: _____

Kind of movie: _____

What it's about: _____

Who likes it: _____

B. Write about the movie you chose.

EXAMPLE:

> <u>Monsoon Wedding</u> is a romantic comedy. It's funny and sad. In the movie, a young woman marries a man she doesn't know. Women love this movie!

Project Idea
Movie Guide
Make a guide to the class's favorite movies.

6 | Do you like to eat out?

1 VOCABULARY: *Fun things to do*

A. YOU FIRST. *Do you prefer to* _____ *or* _____? Check (✓) your answers.

1.

☐ go to the movies   ☐ stay home and watch videos

2.

☐ hang out with a few friends   ☐ go to a party

3.

☐ go to a concert   ☐ go to a sports event

4.

☐ eat out at a restaurant   ☐ eat take-out food at home

B. 🎧 **PRONUNCIATION.** Listen and practice the questions above.

C. TALK AROUND. Interview three classmates. Check (✓) their answers in the chart.

Do you prefer to . . .	_____ (name)	_____ (name)	_____ (name)
1. go to the movies **OR** stay home and watch videos?	☐ ☐	☐ ☐	☐ ☐
2. hang out with a few friends **OR** go to a party?	☐ ☐	☐ ☐	☐ ☐
3. go to a concert **OR** go to a sports event?	☐ ☐	☐ ☐	☐ ☐
4. eat out at a restaurant **OR** eat take-out food at home?	☐ ☐	☐ ☐	☐ ☐

> Do you prefer to go to the movies or stay home and watch videos?

> I prefer to stay home and watch videos.

> Really? Why's that?

> Because it's relaxing... and cheap!

D. REPORT. Tell your classmates about one thing in your chart.

> _____ prefers _____ because _____.

A. LOOK/THINK/GUESS. What are Nick and Gabby talking about?

B. 🎧 **MODEL CONVERSATION.** Listen and practice.

Gabby: What do you want to do tonight? Do you want to watch a video?

Nick: Not really. I don't like to stay home on Friday nights. It's boring.

Gabby: Well, how about a concert?

Nick: A concert? What kind of music?

Gabby: Let's see . . . There's a reggae band at The Super Club.

Nick: I don't know. The Super Club is always crowded and smoky.

Gabby: Well, there's a jazz concert at Jack's Place.

Nick: That sounds fun, but I'm broke.

Gabby: That's OK. It's on me!

> **IDIOM**
>
> **I'm broke.** = I don't have any money.
>
> **It's on me.** = I will pay.

C. 🎧 **ACTIVE LISTENING.** Listen to two more conversations. What do the people decide to do? Check (✓) the answers.

Conversation #1 *They decide to . . .*	Conversation #2 *They decide to . . .*
☐ go to a movie	☐ go to a concert
☐ stay home and watch videos	☐ go to a basketball game
☐ go out to eat	☐ hang out at home

QUESTIONS

Do	you your friends	**like to** **want to**	eat out? go dancing? watch videos?
Does	your partner your sister		
Do	you	**prefer to**	go to a concert or go dancing?
Does	your partner		go to the movies or watch videos?

ANSWERS

Yes,	I they	do.
No,		don't.
Yes,	he she	does.
No,		doesn't.
I **prefer to**		go dancing.
He **prefers to** She		go to the movies.

More
Pronunciation
Practice:

Reduced form of "want to"
Turn to page 88.

B. GET IT RIGHT. Write the questions. Then ask a partner the questions.

1. you /like/watch/sumo wrestling?
   Do you like to watch sumo wrestling?

2. you/want/eat out?
   _____

3. your teacher /like/go dancing?
   _____

4. you/prefer/eat pizza or spaghetti?
   _____

5. you/want/go to the movies/tonight?
   _____

6. you/prefer/go to the movies at night or in the afternoon?
   _____

7. your friends/like/chat online?
   _____

8. a lot of people in this class/like/play soccer?
   _____

C. YOUR IDEAS. Write more questions with *like to*, *want to* or *prefer to*. Then ask a partner your questions.

Do you like to _____?

Do you want to _____?

Do you prefer to _____ or _____?

A. 🎧 **LISTEN and ADD.** Listen and write the missing words. Then practice with a partner.

1. A: Do you want to eat out
tonight?

B: _____?

A: Yeah.

B: Sure. I'd love to.

2. A: Would you like to go
dancing tonight?

B: _____?

A: Yes.

B: Sorry, I can't. I'm busy.

3. A: Hey, let's go out.

B: _____?

A: Yeah. I want to try that
noodle restaurant.

B: Okay.

B. FINISH IT. Complete the conversation. Then
practice with a partner.

A: Do you want to _____?

B: _____?

A: Yeah.

B: _____

A. YOU FIRST. List three fun things you want to do this weekend.

1. _____

2. _____

3. _____

B. PAIR UP and TALK. A: Invite **B** to do something. **B:** Repeat to check understanding.
A and **B:** Try to agree on something to do.

Hey, do you want to do something this weekend?

Do something? Like what?

Let's go to a classical music concert.

I don't like classical music. Do you want to go dancing?

C. PRESENT and WATCH. You and your Partner: Present the role play to another pair.
Your Classmates: Watch the role play. How did they do? Check (✓) your answers.

Did . . .	Yes	No	Not sure
A invite **B** to do something?	☐	☐	☐
B repeat to check understanding?	☐	☐	☐
A and **B** agree on what to do?	☐	☐	☐

Free Time Around the World

► Fore!

In Japan, people love to play golf. Every day, 1,250,000 Japanese people either play golf or hit golf balls in indoor driving ranges. The population of Japan is about 125,000,000 so that's a lot of people!

▼ The Great Outdoors

People in Brazil want to be outdoors in their free time. They like to go to the beach, do water sports, watch or play soccer, hike, bike, or just hang out. Brazilians also love to use their cell phones. Brazil has the largest number of cell phone users in the world!

◄ Cut!

People in India like to watch movies. Every day, 15 million Indians go to the movies. There are 13,000 movie screens in India. India's film industry is the biggest in the world.

► Checkmate!

What's the second most popular activity in Canada? Chess! More than 20 percent of Canadians say they like to play chess. This is especially true for Canadians between 15 and 30 years old. Chess is a perfect activity for those cold Canadian winter days.

READ ABOUT IT

A. Complete the sentences.

1. One percent of _____ people play _____.

2. The largest number of cell phone users is in _____.

3. Indians like to _____ in their free time.

4. _____ is a popular activity in Canada.

B. Read your sentences to a partner.

TALK ABOUT IT

Pairs. Take turns asking and answering questions.

1. Which activities are expensive?

2. What's a good family activity?

3. Which activities do you like to do? Why?

4. What are some other outdoor activities?

5. Your question: _____

WRITE ABOUT IT

A. Choose an activity that you like to do. Make notes.

Name of activity: _____

Place that you like to do it: _____

Why you like to do it: _____

B. Write about the event you chose.

EXAMPLE:

I like to go to the beach in my free time. The beach is near my house. At the beach I swim and I read. I like it because I get exercise and I relax.

Project Idea
Brochure
Make an illustrated brochure with ideas for ways to spend free time in your area.

Review of Units 4-6

1 CONVERSATION

You and your partner want to do something together tonight. Write a conversation. Use two or three words or phrases from each column, then practice.

COLUMN 1	COLUMN 2
want to	movie
prefer to	concert
like to	eat out
like	go to a party
what kind	watch a video

2 INFORMATION GAP

Student A, look at the information below. Student B, turn to page 84.

STUDENT A

A. Ask your partner about each activity in the chart below. Write *Yes* or *No* in the chart. Then answer your partner's questions.

    A: Do you <u>like to listen to rap music?</u>   B: <u>Yes, I do. I think it's great.</u>

B. Take turns asking questions about David and Nina. Write *Yes* or *No* in the chart.

	like to listen to rap music?	like to watch horror movies?	like to go dancing?	like to play volleyball?	want to eat out tonight?
Do you . . .	_____	_____	_____	_____	_____
Does David . . .	Yes	_____	Yes	No	_____
Does Nina . . .	_____	No	_____	_____	Yes

C. Write four sentences about the people in the chart.

Both David and Nina _____.

Nina _____, but David doesn't.

My partner and Nina _____.

My partner and David _____.

3 GAME

Play the game with a partner.

A. Write your name on a small piece of paper.

B. Move your paper by flipping a coin.

 = one space    = two spaces

C. Answer the question or do the task on the space.

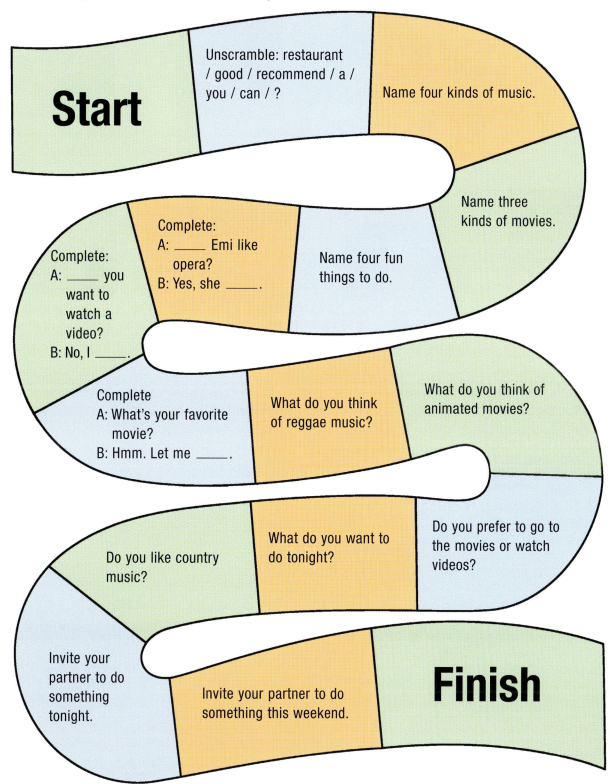

Start

Unscramble: restaurant / good / recommend / a / you / can / ?

Name four kinds of music.

Name three kinds of movies.

Complete:
A: _____ Emi like opera?
B: Yes, she _____.

Name four fun things to do.

Complete:
A: _____ you want to watch a video?
B: No, I _____.

Complete
A: What's your favorite movie?
B: Hmm. Let me _____.

What do you think of reggae music?

What do you think of animated movies?

Do you like country music?

What do you want to do tonight?

Do you prefer to go to the movies or watch videos?

Invite your partner to do something tonight.

Invite your partner to do something this weekend.

Finish

7 When do you have lunch?

1 VOCABULARY: *Daily routines*

A. YOU FIRST. Are these sentences true for *you*? Check (✓) *yes* or *no*.

1. I usually get up before 6:00 A.M.
☐ Yes ☐ No

2. I eat a big breakfast.
☐ Yes ☐ No

3. I leave home at 7:30 in the morning.
☐ Yes ☐ No

4. I have lunch around 12:15 P.M.
☐ Yes ☐ No

5. I get home about 6:00 P.M.
☐ Yes ☐ No

6. I check my e-mail after dinner.
☐ Yes ☐ No

7. I watch TV in the evening.
☐ Yes ☐ No

8. I usually go to bed after midnight.
☐ Yes ☐ No

B. 🎧 **PRONUNCIATION.** Listen and practice the sentences above.

C. TALK AROUND. Ask your classmates the questions below. Complete each sentence with a classmates' name.

Questions
1. Do you usually get up before 6:00 A.M?
2. Do you usually eat a small breakfast?
3. Do you leave home after 10:00 A.M.?
4. Do you have a big lunch?
5. Do you check your e-mail after dinner?
6. Do you go to bed after midnight?

Classmate's name
1. _____ gets up before 6:00 A.M.
2. _____ eats a small breakfast.
3. _____ leaves home after 10:00 A.M.
4. _____ has a big lunch.
5. _____ checks e-mail after dinner.
6. _____ goes to bed after midnight.

D. REPORT. Tell your classmates about one person in your chart.

> _____ has a big lunch.

A. 🎧 **FIRST LISTENING.** Check (✓) the correct information for each person.

	Chris *Australia*		Yu Chen *Taiwan*		Gina *Mexico*	
Gets up at . . .	☐ 6 A.M.	☐ 7 A.M.	☐ 7 A.M.	☐ 8 A.M.	☐ 7 A.M.	☐ 8:30 A.M.
	☐ 8 A.M.	☐ 9 A.M.	☐ 9:30 A.M.	☐ 6 A.M.	☐ 9 A.M.	☐ 6:30 A.M.
Eats breakfast?	☐ Yes	☐ No	☐ Yes	☐ No	☐ Yes	☐ No
Starts work at . . .	☐ 7 A.M.	☐ 8 A.M.	☐ 8 A.M.	☐ 9 A.M.	☐ 9 A.M.	☐ 10 A.M.
	☐ 9 A.M.	☐ 8:30 A.M.	☐ 9:30 A.M.	☐ 10 A.M.	☐ 8 A.M.	☐ 11 A.M.
Gets home in the evening . . .	☐ early		☐ at 7 P.M.		☐ at 7 P.M.	
	☐ around 8 P.M.		☐ at dinner time		☐ late	
	☐ at midnight		☐ late		☐ at midnight	

B. 🎧 **SECOND LISTENING.** Circle the mistakes.

	True	False
1. Chris works ten hours straight, four days on and four days off.	☐	☐
2. Yu Chen reads the newspaper on-line.	☐	☐
3. In the morning, Yu Chen studies for the national university entrance exam.	☐	☐
4. Gina is busy 24–7.	☐	☐
5. Gina works at a hotel.	☐	☐
6. Gina goes out to dinner with her co-workers.	☐	☐

> **IDIOM**
>
> **24–7** = All the time (24 hours a day, seven days a week).

C. PAIR UP AND TALK. Ask a partner the questions.

> What do you have in common with _____?
>
> Chris   Yu Chen   Gina

> We both _____.

> Oh, really? That's interesting.

A. 🎧 **PRONUNCIATION.** Listen and practice the questions and answers.

QUESTIONS					ANSWERS		
When What time	do	you	get up?		I	get up	at 7:30.
	does	he she		→	He She	gets up	early.
What	do	you	do	in the morning? in the afternoon? after dinner?	I	go to class. study. watch TV.
	does does	he she		→	He She	goes to class. studies. watches TV.

More
Pronunciation
Practice

Reduced forms of
"wh-" questions.
Turn to page 89.

B. GET IT RIGHT. Find the mistake and write the correct question. Then ask a partner the questions.

1. **Incorrect:** When you usually have breakfast?
   Correct: *When do you usually have breakfast?*

2. **Incorrect:** When do your best friend usually study?
   Correct: _____

3. **Incorrect:** What time does you get up?
   Correct: _____

4. **Incorrect:** What your teacher usually do at the beginning of class?
   Correct: _____

5. **Incorrect:** What time you has lunch?
   Correct: _____

6. **Incorrect:** You usually watch TV when?
   Correct: _____

7. **Incorrect:** What you do in the evening?
   Correct: _____

8. **Incorrect:** When does you usually check your e-mail?
   Correct: _____

C. YOUR IDEAS. Write more questions with *when* and *what time*.
Ask a partner your questions.

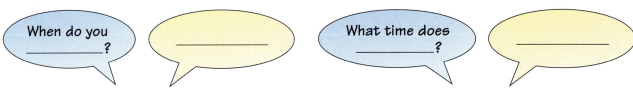

When do you _____ ?   _____   What time does _____ ?   _____

4 CONVERSATION STRATEGY: *Showing you are listening*

A. 🎧 PRONUNCIATION. Listen and practice the phrases.

> Uh huh.

> I see.

> Right.

B. 🎧 LISTEN and ADD. Write the missing expressions. Then practice with a partner.

1. A: What time does the movie begin?

B: The early show is at 7:00 and the late show is at 9:00.

A: _____.

Thank you.

2. A: What time does the mall open and close?

B: It opens at 10 A.M. on weekdays and 9 A.M. on weekends.

A: _____.

B: And it closes at 10 P.M.

A: _____. Thanks.

5 TALKATHON: *Living for the weekend*

A. YOU FIRST. Make notes about your weekday and weekend routines.

	Weekdays	Weekends
Morning		
Afternoon		
Evening		

B. PAIR UP and TALK. Ask your partner about weekday and weekend routines. Remember to show you are listening.

> What do you do on weekday mornings?

> Well, I get up at . . .

> Uh huh. And what do you do on weekend mornings?

> I sleep late.

C. REPORT. Get together with another pair and tell them about your partner.

Good Luck Routines

Many people have good luck routines. Do you?

▼ **Frankie Muniz,** TV and movie star, has a good luck routine. He says special words about a hundred times. He does this before he acts, flies, or even drives a car. What words does he say? He's not telling!

▲ Movie star **Nicole Kidman** has a pair of very special good luck earrings. She always wears them to award ceremonies like the Oscars.

◄ **Mike Harmon,** the race car driver, doesn't have any good luck routines. However, he thinks that some things bring him bad luck. For example, he doesn't like to drive green cars. Also, he doesn't like people to eat peanuts near his car before a race.

▲ Some **athletes** have good luck routines. For example, soccer players often bounce the ball an even (2, 4, 6, etc.) number of times before a game.

READ ABOUT IT

A. Read and complete the sentences.

1. Nicole Kidman wears _____ for good luck.

2. Frankie Muniz says special _____ many times.

3. Soccer players like to _____ the _____ 2, 4, 6, or 8 times before a game.

4. Mike Harmon thinks that some things bring him _____ luck.

B. Read your sentences to a partner.

TALK ABOUT IT

Pairs. Take turns asking and answering questions.

1. What do you think brings you good luck?

2. What do you think brings you bad luck?

3. Your question: _____

WRITE ABOUT IT

A. Make notes about two more good luck and/or bad luck routines. If you don't have any, write about the good/bad luck routines of someone you know.

Description of each routine: Reason for each routine:

1. _____   _____

   _____   _____

2. _____   _____

   _____   _____

B. Write about your good and/or bad luck routines or the routines of someone you know.

EXAMPLE:

> I have two good luck routines. One on the first day of every month I say, "Rabbit, rabbit, rabbit," before I say anything else. This brings me good luck all month. Also, on my birthday, I blow out the candles on my birthday cake and make a wish, but I never tell anyone my wish. It's bad luck to tell your wish.

Project Idea

Internet Research: Good Luck
Find out what people think brings them good luck and bad luck in another country. Make a report with examples and illustrations.

1 VOCABULARY: *Healthy and unhealthy habits*

A. YOU FIRST. *Do you* _____? Check (✓) yes or no.

1. eat a lot of junk food
☐ yes ☐ no

2. get enough sleep
☐ yes ☐ no

3. smoke
☐ yes ☐ no

4. take vitamins
☐ yes ☐ no

5. exercise every day
☐ yes ☐ no

6. drink a lot of soda
☐ yes ☐ no

7. spend a lot of time outdoors
☐ yes ☐ no

8. eat vegetables every day
☐ yes ☐ no

B. 🎧 **PRONUNCIATION.** Listen and practice the questions above.

C. PAIR UP and TALK. Interview a partner.

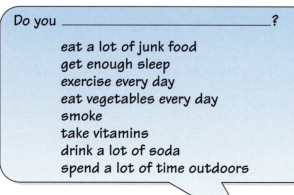

Do you _____?

eat a lot of junk food
get enough sleep
exercise every day
eat vegetables every day
smoke
take vitamins
drink a lot of soda
spend a lot of time outdoors

No, I don't.

Really?

Yes, I do.

That's interesting.

D. REPORT. Tell your classmates one thing about your partner.

A. LOOK/THINK/GUESS. Where are Gabby and Mike? What are they talking about?

B. 🎧 MODEL CONVERSATION. Listen and practice.

Gabby: Hi Mike, how are you?

Mike: I'm fine. Boy, you look really great!

Gabby: Thanks. I'm really into exercise these days. I go to the gym a lot.

Mike: Really? How often do you go?

Gabby: Every day, usually.

Mike: That's impressive.

Gabby: And I try to eat a good diet. No soda; no junk food; just lots of healthy stuff, like vegetables.

Mike: Not me. I don't like to cook and I hate vegetables. I live on instant noodles and diet soda.

> **IDIOMS**
>
> **I'm into** = I really like
> **I live on** = I eat a lot of

C. 🎧 ACTIVE LISTENING. Listen to two more conversations. Check (✓) *true* or *false*.

Conversation #1	True	False
1. Anna wants to run in a marathon.	☐	☐
2. Running is easy for Anna.	☐	☐
3. Anna smokes a lot.	☐	☐
Conversation #2	**True**	**False**
1. George is very tired.	☐	☐
2. George usually gets enough sleep.	☐	☐
3. George has an exam today.	☐	☐

A. 🎧 PRONUNCIATION. Listen and practice the questions and answers.

QUESTIONS				ANSWERS
How often	do	you they	exercise? eat junk food? drink soda? get enough sleep? play a sport?	→
	does	your sister your friend		Every day. Four times a week. Once a month. Twice a year. Never.

More Pronunciation Practice

Sentence stress.
Turn to page 89.

B. GET IT RIGHT. Unscramble the questions. Then ask a partner the questions.

1. How/you/often/do/eat out?

   _____

   _____

2. How/your/exercise/often/does/best friend?

   _____

   _____

3. How/check e-mail/friends/often/your/do?

   _____

   _____

4. How/you/get/sleep/do/enough/often?

   _____

   _____

5. How/your/the movies/often/do/friends/go to?

   _____

   _____

6. How/surf the Internet/often/you/do?

   _____

   _____

C. YOUR IDEAS. Write more questions with *How often*. Ask a partner your questions.

How often do you _____?

_____

How often does _____?

_____

4 CONVERSATION STRATEGY: Asking follow-up questions

A. 🎧 PRONUNCIATION. Listen and practice the questions.

> When do you go to bed?

> What kind of food?

> What is your favorite movie?

B. 🎧 LISTEN and ADD. Listen and write the follow-up questions. Then practice with a partner.

1. A: Do you get enough exercise?

B: Yes, I think so.

A: _____

_____ ?

B: I run.

2. A: Do you sleep late?

B: No, not really.

A: Oh. _____

_____ ?

B: Around 7:00.

3. A: Do you watch a lot of TV?

B: Yes, I do.

A: Really? _____

_____ ?

B: The Comedy Hour.

5 TALKATHON: Do you have a healthy lifestyle?

A. DISCUSS and DECIDE. With a partner, list some things that are . . .

Good for your health	Not good for your health

B. PAIR UP and TALK. Change partners. Ask your new partner about your list. Then ask a follow-up question.

> Do you exercise?

> Yes, I do.

> What kind of exercise?

> I usually _____ .

C. REPORT. Tell your classmates about your partner.

Living Longer

Follow these tips to live a long and healthy life!

▼ Laughter is good for both our minds and our bodies. It helps us relax. Because it uses many muscles, laughing is a kind of exercise. Average adults laugh about 17 times a day. How often do you laugh?

▲ Meditation can add years to your life. Meditating for 15 to 30 minutes a day relaxes you and reduces the risk of heart attacks. Everyone has 15 minutes, right?

▲ People who live a long life have lots of friends. But it isn't enough to have friends. You need to spend time with your friends. How much time do you spend with your friends?

◀ Most people who live a long time don't eat one or two big meals a day. They eat five or six small meals a day. Of course, they don't eat a lot of food each time they eat. How often do you eat?

READ ABOUT IT

A. Read and complete the sentences.

1. _____ only takes 15 to 30 minutes a day to reduce the risk of heart attacks.

2. _____ is a kind of exercise.

3. Laughter and meditation help to _____ you.

4. Most people who live a long time eat _____ meals a day.

B. Read your sentences to a partner.

TALK ABOUT IT

Pairs. Take turns asking and answering questions.

1. Do you laugh a lot?

2. How many times a day do you usually eat?

3. What do you do to relax?

4. How much time do you spend with friends every week?

5. Your question: _____?

WRITE ABOUT IT

A. Do you follow any of the tips for living longer? Take notes on the tips you follow.

Tips you follow	Details (What? When? How often?)
_____	_____
_____	_____
_____	_____

B. Write about the tip or tips you follow.

EXAMPLE:

I do a lot of things that make me laugh. For example, I often go to comedies. I also watch funny programs on TV and I read the comics in the newspaper every day. I also spend a lot of time with my friends. Why? Because they make me laugh, too.

Project Idea

Oral history: The secret to a long life

Interview five people who are more than 80 years old. Ask, "What helps a person to live a long life?" Write a report about their answers.

9 Did you go to the gym?

1 VOCABULARY: *Weekend activities*

A. YOU FIRST. What did *you* do last weekend? Check (✓) *yes* or *no*.

1. I got up early.
☐ yes   ☐ no

2. I went shopping.
☐ yes   ☐ no

3. I did the laundry.
☐ yes   ☐ no

4. I went to the gym.
☐ yes   ☐ no

5. I played computer games.
☐ yes   ☐ no

6. I took a nap.
☐ yes   ☐ no

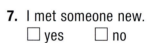

7. I met someone new.
☐ yes   ☐ no

8. I stayed up late.
☐ yes   ☐ no

B. 🎧 **PRONUNCIATION.** Listen and practice the sentences above.

C. PAIR UP and TALK. Interview a partner. Check (✓) your partner's answers.

> Did you _____ last weekend?
>
> get up late   play computer games
> go shopping   take a nap
> do the laundry   meet someone new
> go to the gym   stay up late

Yes, I did.

No, I didn't.

D. REPORT. Tell your classmates one thing about your partner.

A. LOOK/THINK/GUESS. Where are Nick and Emma? How was Emma's weekend?

B. 🎧 **MODEL CONVERSATION.** Listen and practice.

Nick: Hi, Emma. How was your weekend?

Emma: Well, Saturday was nothing special. But Sunday was ==something else!==

Nick: Really? What did you do?

Emma: Well, Sunday afternoon I went to the gym with Joan.

Nick: I know Joan—your friend from high school, right?

Emma: That's right. Anyway, I met her friend Antonio. He's really nice.

Nick: Oh, you met someone new?

Emma: Well, yeah. Actually, we went for a walk and talked. We have a lot in common.

Nick: That's interesting. Go on . . .

Emma: Then we went out to dinner. After dinner we went out dancing.

Nick: ==No wonder== you look so tired!

> **IDIOMS**
>
> It was **something else.** = It was special.
> **No wonder** = That's the reason

C. 🎧 **ACTIVE LISTENING.** What did Jeff do on his day off? Check (✔) the answers.

1.	When did Jeff get up?	☐ early	☐ late	☐ I don't know.
2.	What did he do?	☐ He went to the gym.	☐ He went to a movie.	☐ He did his laundry.
3.	Who did he meet later?	☐ a friend	☐ someone from work	☐ his sister
4.	What did they do?	☐ They watched TV.	☐ They ate pizza.	☐ They went shopping.

A. 🎧 **PRONUNCIATION.** Listen and practice the questions and answers.

QUESTIONS				ANSWERS	
Did	you	get up early today?	→	Yes, I **did**.	I **got up** at 6.
	she	go shopping yesterday?		No she **didn't**.	She **went shopping** this morning.
	he	eat out last week?		Yes, he **did**.	He **ate** at an Indian restaurant.
	they	watch TV last night?		No, they **didn't**.	They **watched** a video.

B. GET IT RIGHT. Complete the answers. Then practice with a partner.

More Pronunciation Practice

"-ed" endings
Turn to page 90.

1. Did your brother watch TV last night?

   Yes, he _____. He _____ the news.

2. Did you have a big breakfast this morning?

   No, I _____. I only _____ coffee.

3. Did you get to class on time today?

   No, I _____. I _____ here a little late.

4. Did you go to the movies last month?

   Yes, I _____. I _____ to a few movies last month.

5. Did Emma take a nap yesterday?

   Yes, she _____. She _____ a nap in the afternoon.

6. Did they eat out last week?

   Yes, they _____. They _____ out on Wednesday.

Regular Verbs	
talk	→ talked
play	→ played
watch	→ watched
study	→ studied

Irregular Verbs*	
get	→ got
go	→ went
do	→ did
meet	→ met
eat	→ ate
take	→ took
have	→ had

*see page 100 for more irregular verbs

C. YOUR IDEAS. Write more questions with *did*. Then ask a partner your questions.

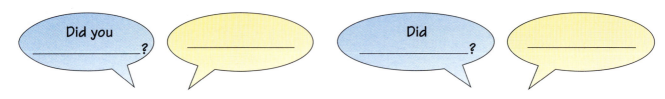

Did you _____?

_____

Did _____?

_____

4 CONVERSATION STRATEGY: *Turning the conversation around*

A. 🎧 **LISTEN and ADD.** Listen and write the missing words. Then practice with a partner.

1. A: Did you watch the TV news last night?

B: Yes, I did. _____?

A: No, I was too busy.

2. A: Do you usually watch the news on TV?

B: No, I don't. _____?

A: Yes, I always watch the channel 6 news.

B. 🎧 **FINISH IT.** Complete the conversations. Then practice with a partner.

1. A: Did you go to the gym yesterday?

B: _____. Did you?

A: _____.

2. A: Do you usually exercise in the morning?

B: _____. Do you?

A: _____.

5 TALKATHON: *Last week BINGO*

A. YOU FIRST. For the last five days, list one thing you did each day.

Day of the week	One thing I did	Classmate who did the same thing

B. TALK AROUND. Find a classmate who did the same thing. Write the person's name in the chart. When you find someone for each day, say "Bingo!"

Did you get up late on Sunday?

Yes, I did. Did you?

C. REPORT. Tell one thing you and a classmate both did.

Weekend Goals and Accomplishments

What did you plan to do this weekend? Did you accomplish your goals?

▼ **Dr. Natalie Ford**   I wanted to grade all these exams and plan my lessons, but I didn't find the time to do both. I planned my lessons, but I didn't correct my exams. Instead, I played tennis and went to the beach with my kids. I had a great time! I'm very busy now, though.

▲ **Kevin Madden**   Let's see. I planned to sleep a lot, play basketball, and hang out with my friends. But I only did one of those things. I didn't play much basketball or hang out with my friends because I had a lot of homework. So, I just did my homework. I slept a lot, too!

◄ **Soo-Young Park**
I planned to study, but I didn't. Instead, I visited some friends. We had a great time together. We ate out at a nice restaurant then went to a party. But now I have to study!

► **Andrew Colstanza**   It was a great weekend. I accomplished a lot. I did some work and washed my car. I also did the laundry. I feel really great! Now I'm ready for Monday.

READ ABOUT IT

A. Complete the sentences with a name or a number.

1. _____ and _____ accomplished only one goal.

2. _____ people had a great weekend.

3. _____ accomplished all of his goals.

4. _____ and _____ have a lot of work to do now.

5. _____ and _____ are ready for Monday.

B. Read your sentences to a partner.

TALK ABOUT IT

Pairs. Take turns asking and answering questions.

1. Which person do you think had the best weekend? Why?

2. Do you usually make weekend plans?

3. Do you usually do everything you planned to do on the weekend? If no, why not?

4. Your question: _____?

WRITE ABOUT IT

A. Complete the charts about last weekend.

Things I planned to do	Did I do it?		Other things I did
1.	☐ Yes	☐ No	
2.	☐ Yes	☐ No	
3.	☐ Yes	☐ No	
4.	☐ Yes	☐ No	

B. Write about your weekend.

EXAMPLE:

I had lots of plans for my weekend. I wanted to do my laundry and clean my bedroom. I also planned to go to a movie with a friend. My washing machine broke, so I didn't do my laundry. I cleaned my bedroom, though. My friend got sick, so I didn't go to a movie. I stayed home and read a book instead. I didn't accomplish all my goals, but I had a good weekend anyway.

Project Idea

Class newspaper: Memorable weekends

Interview a classmate about a memorable weekend (good or bad). Write a short report for a class newspaper.

Review of Units 7-9

1 CONVERSATION

A. Pairs. Have a conversation about your weekend.

A: How was your weekend?

B: It was _____.
  I _____ on Saturday.

A: Really? How often do you _____?

B: Hmm . . . about _____.
  So, how was your weekend?

B: It was _____.
  On Saturday I _____.

A: That's interesting. What did you do on Sunday?

B: I _____ and _____.

2 INTERVIEW

A. Pairs. Choose a topic from the box. Write questions, then interview your partner about the topic.

Daily Routines	Healthy and Unhealthy Habits	Weekend Activities

EXAMPLE:

Daily Routines
1. What time do you go to bed?
2. What time do you get up?
3.
4.

B. Tell your classmates about your partner.

3 GAME

Play the game with a partner.

A. Write your name on a small piece of paper.

B. Move your paper by flipping a coin.

 = one space　　　　 = two spaces

C. Answer the question or do the task on the space.

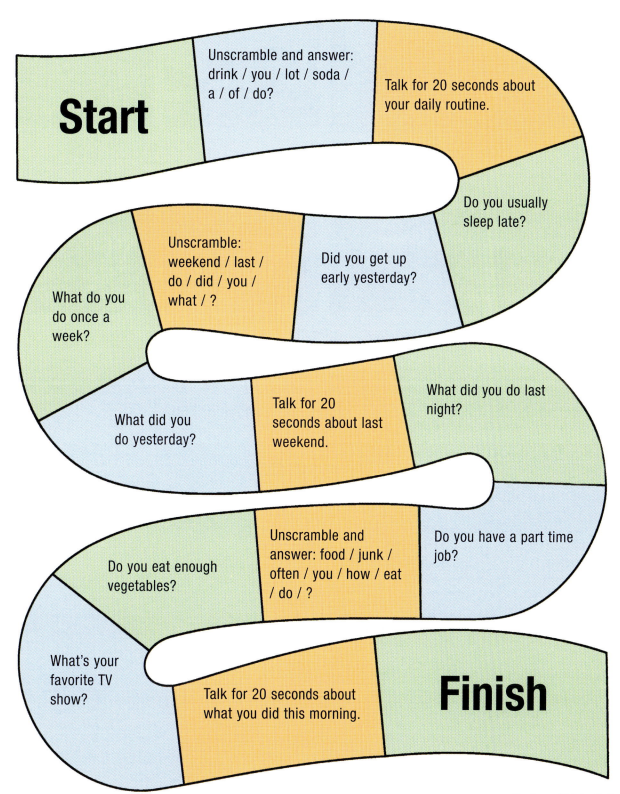

Start

Unscramble and answer:
drink / you / lot / soda /
a / of / do?

Talk for 20 seconds about
your daily routine.

Do you usually
sleep late?

Unscramble:
weekend / last /
do / did / you /
what / ?

Did you get up
early yesterday?

What do you
do once a
week?

What did you
do yesterday?

Talk for 20
seconds about last
weekend.

What did you do last
night?

Do you eat enough
vegetables?

Unscramble and
answer: food / junk /
often / you / how / eat
/ do / ?

Do you have a part time
job?

What's your
favorite TV
show?

Talk for 20 seconds about
what you did this morning.

Finish

10 Is there an ATM around here?

1 VOCABULARY: *Places*

A. YOU FIRST. *Is there a _____ in your neighborhood?* Check (✓) yes or no.

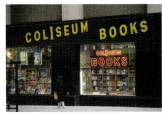

1. bank
☐ yes ☐ no

2. convenience store
☐ yes ☐ no

3. gas station
☐ yes ☐ no

4. bookstore
☐ yes ☐ no

5. drugstore
☐ yes ☐ no

6. department store
☐ yes ☐ no

7. shopping mall
☐ yes ☐ no

8. coffee shop
☐ yes ☐ no

B. 🎧 PRONUNCIATION. Listen and practice the questions above.

C. PAIR UP and TALK. Interview a partner. Remember to ask follow-up questions.

> Is there a _____ in your neighborhood?
>
> | | |
> |---|---|
> | bank | convenience store |
> | gas station | bookstore |
> | drugstore | department store |
> | shopping mall | coffee shop |

Yes, there is.

No, there isn't.

Follow-up Questions

Did you go there often?

Did you go there last week?

Which one?

_____?

D. REPORT. Tell your classmates one thing about your partner's neighborhood.

A. LOOK/THINK/GUESS. Where are Gabby and Nick? What questions do you think they are asking?

B. 🎧 MODEL CONVERSATION. Listen and practice.

Clerk: Can I help you?

Gabby: Yes. Is there an easy way to get downtown?

Clerk: Sure. You can take the bus or the subway.
        Where do you want to go?

Gabby: To the Art Museum.

Clerk: It's five stops on the subway. You take the Blue Line
        to Center City and change to the Red Line.

Gabby: Thanks. Oh, one more question: Is there an ATM
        around here?

Clerk: There are two. One is across from the newsstand.
        The other is next to the drugstore.

Gabby: Thanks.

Clerk: No problem.

> **IDIOM**
>
> **No problem** = You're welcome.

C. 🎧 ACTIVE LISTENING. What does the person ask for? What does the clerk suggest?

	The person asks for . . .		The clerk suggests . . .	
Conversation #1	☐ a bus	☐ a taxi	☐ the subway	☐ a taxi
Conversation #2	☐ a bank	☐ a department store	☐ a drugstore	☐ an ATM

A. 🎧 **PRONUNCIATION.** Listen and practice the questions and answers.

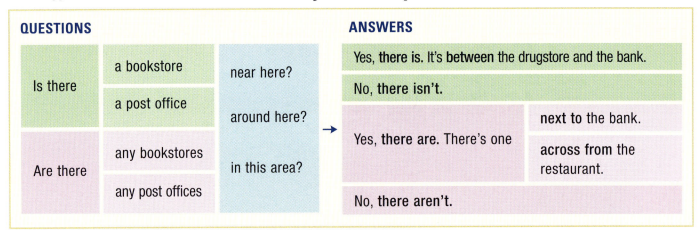

QUESTIONS			ANSWERS
Is there	a bookstore	near here?	Yes, **there is.** It's **between** the drugstore and the bank.
	a post office	around here?	No, **there isn't.**
Are there	any bookstores	in this area?	Yes, **there are.** There's one — **next to** the bank. / **across from** the restaurant.
	any post offices		No, **there aren't.**

B. GET IT RIGHT. Look at the map. Complete the questions and answers. Then practice with a partner.

More Pronunciation Practice

Initial 'th' sounds. Turn to page 91.

22

1. A: *Is there* a drugstore in the area?

B: Yes, there's one *next to* the bookstore.

2. A: _____ a movie theater around here?

B: Yes, there _____. It's _____ the department store.

3. A: _____ any restaurants near here?

B: Yes, there_____. There's a good restaurant _____ the_____ and the _____.

4. A: _____ a CD store around here?

B: No, there _____.

5. A: _____ a gas station in the area?

B: Yes, there _____. _____ one _____ the bank.

6. A: _____ any coffee shops around here?

B: Yes, there _____. There's a nice one _____ the gas station.

C. YOUR IDEAS. Write more questions with *is there* and *are there*. Then ask a partner your questions.

Is there _____ near here?

_____

Are there _____ near your house?

_____

A. 🎧 **PRONUNCIATION.** Listen and practice the questions.

> Excuse me?

> Could you please say that again?

B. 🎧 **LISTEN AND ADD.** Write the missing questions. Then practice with a partner.

1. A: Is there an ATM around here?

B: _____?

A: Is there an ATM near here?

B: Yes, there's one across the street.

A: Thanks.

2. A: Is there a mailbox around here?

B: _____?

A: Is there a mailbox nearby?

B: Yes, I think there's one near the subway station.

A: Thanks.

A. YOU FIRST. Draw a map of the area around your school. Label places on the map.

B. PAIR UP and TALK. Take turns playing the roles below. Remember to ask for repetition.
A: You are a visitor to B's school. Ask B three questions about the area around the school.
B: Use your map to answer A's questions.

> Is there a _____ around here?

> Excuse me?

> Is there a _____ near here?

> Sure, there's one _____.

C. PRESENT and WATCH.

You and Your Partner: Present the roleplay to another pair.

Your Classmates: Watch the roleplay. How did they do? Check (✓) your answers.

Did . . .	Yes	No	Not sure
A ask *B* about three places?	☐	☐	☐
A or *B* ask for repetition?	☐	☐	☐
B answer *A's* questions?	☐	☐	☐

It's a great neighborhood!

◄ We moved to Westfield because it's beautiful and quiet. There are lots of cows and sheep everywhere. We don't have many neighbors, but we like it that way. There's a post office and a small supermarket here and not much else.

◄ Park Towers is a great place for singles and couples. All the apartments are new and have great views of the city. We live on the 35th floor! Most people who live here work nearby. The nightlife is terrific. It's a wonderful place, but you can't have pets or children here.

▲ We live on Calle Real and we love it. It's a very quiet neighborhood. It's also very pretty. There's a nice shopping center nearby with a few good restaurants. Best of all, lots of families with young children live in this area.

◄ I live in University Place. This is a great neighborhood for students. It's not very pretty, but it's cheap. The university is nearby. There's a lot to do around here. There's a good bookstore nearby, and a convenience store next to the bookstore. There is also a bus stop across the street from my apartment.

READ ABOUT IT

A. Complete the sentences.

1. University Place is a good neighborhood for _____ because _____ .

2. There aren't many families in _____ .

3. Park Towers is a great neighborhood for _____ .

4. Calle Real is good for _____ because _____ .

6. People who like living in the country like _____ because it is _____ and there _____ .

B. Read your sentences to a partner.

TALK ABOUT IT

Pairs. Take turns asking and answering questions.

1. What do you like about each neighborhood?

2. What do you *not* like about each neighborhood?

3. Which neighborhood do you prefer? Why?

4. Your question: _____ ?

WRITE ABOUT IT

A. Make notes about *your* neighborhood.

Name of your town/city and neighborhood: _____

Kinds of people who live in your neighborhood: _____

Things you like about your neighborhood: _____

Things you don't like about your neighborhood: _____

B. Write about your neighborhood.

EXAMPLE:

I live in Santa Ynez. My neighborhood is called Montevista. There are many families in this neighborhood. This is because there are very good schools in the area. Another good thing about my neighborhood is the beautiful view of the mountains from most of the houses. A bad thing about our neighborhood is there aren't any stores or restaurants nearby.

Project Idea
Neighborhood Guide
Make a "neighborhood guide" for visitors to your city. Include information about what makes different neighborhoods special or interesting.

11 I want to buy a CD.

1 VOCABULARY: *Things to buy*

A. YOU FIRST. *How much did you spend on _____ last month?* Write the amount of money.

1. school or office supplies

_____

2. CD's or DVD's

_____

3. jewelry

_____

4. cosmetics

_____

5. gifts

_____

6. clothing

_____

7. reading material

_____

8. electronic equipment

_____

B. 🎧 **PRONUNCIATION.** Listen and practice the questions above.

C. PAIR UP and TALK. Interview a partner. Ask follow-up questions.

> How much did you spend on _____ last month?
>
> school or office supplies   CDs or DVDs
>
> jewelry   cosmetics
>
> electronic equipment   clothing
>
> reading material   gifts

> I spent _____.

> I didn't buy any _____.

> **Follow-up Questions**
>
> What did you buy?
>
> Where did you buy _____?
>
> _____?

D. REPORT. Tell your classmates one thing about your partner.

A. 🎧 **FIRST LISTENING.** Listen and complete the sentences.

1.

José says that in Mexico, people give gifts on Christmas Eve. They usually give children _____, toys, and _____.

2.

Chung-ja says that in Korea, people give _____, school supplies, and _____ on New Year's Day.

3.

Matt says that his favorite time to give gifts is Valentine's Day. He gives women _____, books, and _____.

B. 🎧 **SECOND LISTENING.** Now listen again. Answer the questions.

1. What did José give his brother and sister for Christmas last year?
He gave his brother _____ and his sister _____.

2. What did Chung-ja get for News Year's when she was a child?
She got _____.

3. What did Matt's girlfriend get him for Valentine's Day last year?
_____.

C. PAIR UP and TALK. Ask a partner about a recent gift. Ask follow-up questions.

What was the gift?	What was the occasion?
Who did you give it to?	Where did you buy it?
Did he/she like it?	

A. 🎧 **PRONUNCIATION.** Listen and practice the sentences.

COUNT NOUNS		NON-COUNT NOUNS	
I bought	a book. three book**s**. some book**s**.	I bought	some jewelry.
I didn't buy	a book. any book**s**.	I didn't buy	any jewelry.
Did you buy	a book? any book**s**?	Did you buy	any jewelry?

Sample count nouns: *notebook, pen, pencil, T-shirt, ring, necklace, ball, net, book, magazine, newspaper*

Sample non-count nouns: *paper, money, jewelry, food, equipment, reading material.*

B. GET IT RIGHT. Circle the correct word.
Check (✔) the sentences that are true for *you*. Then tell a partner.

More
Pronunciation
Practice

Plural "-s" and "-es" endings
Turn to page 92.

	True for Me
1. I want to buy (a / some) CD.	☐
2. I didn't buy (a / any) newspaper last week.	☐
3. My parents gave me (a / some) money last year.	☐
4. I need (a / some) sports equipment.	☐
5. I don't need (a / any) new pens.	☐
6. I ate (a / some) delicious food yesterday.	☐
7. I need to buy (any / some) paper.	☐
8. I don't have (any / some) questions.	☐

C. YOUR IDEAS. Write more questions. Then ask a partner your questions.

Did you buy _____ _____ yesterday?

Do you need to buy _____ _____?

Did you eat _____ _____?

4 CONVERSATION STRATEGY: *Making suggestions*

A. 🎧 **PRONUNCIATION.** Listen and practice the questions.

> What about the mall?

> Why don't you try Mega Mart?

> Why don't you go to Bookland?

B. 🎧 **LISTEN and ADD.** Write the missing words. Then practice with a partner.

1. A: Where's a good place to buy CDs?

B: _____

Amazon?

A: Where's that?

B: It's online.

2. A: Where's a good place to buy men's clothes?

B: _____

Macy's?

A: Macy's? Where's that?

B: It's on 17th Street.

3. A: Where's a good place to buy used books?

B: _____

Powell's Books?

A: Where's Powell's Books?

B: It's across the street.

5 TALKATHON: *Places to shop*

A. YOU FIRST. Make a list of four things you want to buy.

Things I Want to Buy	
1.	3.
2.	4.

B. PAIR UP and TALK. Ask your partner where to buy each thing on your list. Write your partner's suggestions.

> Where's a good place to buy _____?

> Why don't you go to _____?

> Where's that?

> It's _____.

Where to shop

_____
_____
_____
_____

C. REPORT. Tell your classmates about one of your places to shop.

Shopping from Home

Shopping from home is **hot**! It's easy, fun, and fast. Who shops from home? A majority of Internet shoppers are younger than 45 years old, and a majority of them are also catalog shoppers. What do people buy from catalogs and over the Internet? Just imagine you need:

- a book
- some clothes
- a pair of shoes
- some jewelry
- an airline ticket.

> **IDIOM**
>
> **hot** = very popular

Which of these items do you like to shop from home for? If you are like most people, you're happy to buy books over the Internet. In fact, books, videos, and CDs are the things people most often buy online. People also buy lots of airline tickets and gifts over the Internet. Some people use the Internet to buy clothes, too, but catalogs are still more popular than the Internet for clothes shopping. Other popular catalog purchases include things for the home, and electronics. However, people still prefer to shop for shoes and jewelry at stores.

READ ABOUT IT

A. Complete the sentences.

1. _____ and _____ are two kinds of home shopping.

2. Most Internet shoppers are _____.

3. People use _____ more for shopping for clothes.

4. Two things that people don't often buy over the Internet or from catalogs are _____ and _____.

5. The most common things people buy over the Internet are _____, _____, and _____.

B. Read your sentences to a partner.

TALK ABOUT IT

Pairs. Take turns asking and answering questions.

1. Do you ever buy things on the Internet? What things? _____

2. Do you ever buy things from catalogs? What things? _____

3. Do you like to shop in stores? What do you like to shop for? _____

4. What's your favorite way to shop? _____

5. Your question: _____?

WRITE ABOUT IT

A. Make notes about your shopping preferences and habits.

The places you shop at most: _____

The things you like to shop for: _____

The things you hate to shop for: _____

B. Write about your shopping preferences and habits.

EXAMPLE:

> I don't like to shop at stores, so shopping at home is perfect for me. I shop on the Internet or from catalogs when I can. I like shopping for CDs, books, and computer games, but I think shopping for clothes and shoes is boring. I especially hate shopping for food.

Project Idea
Catalog cover
Design the cover and choose a name for a specialty catalog. (Examples: World music CDs, Children's clothes, Sports equipment, Comic books.)

12 That's a nice jacket!

1 VOCABULARY: *Clothes*

A. YOU FIRST. *How often do you wear* _____ *?* Mark the clothing items:

✓✓✓ = Wear a lot   ✓ = Wear once in a while   ✗ = Never wear

1. a dress _____
high heels _____

2. a tie _____ a suit _____

3. a skirt _____ a blouse _____
a sweater _____

4. a fleece jacket _____
casual pants _____
boots _____

5. a sweatshirt _____
jeans _____
athletic shoes _____

6. a T-shirt _____
shorts _____
sandals _____

B. 🎧 **PRONUNCIATION.** Listen and practice the questions above.

C. PAIR UP and TALK. Interview a partner about five of the clothing items above. Remember to ask follow-up questions.

> How often do you wear <u>a tie</u>?

> Once in a while.

> **Follow-up Questions**
>
> When do you wear _____?
>
> Did you wear _____ last week?
>
> Do you like to wear _____?
>
> Why? _____?

D. REPORT. Tell your classmates one thing about your partner.

A. LOOK/THINK/GUESS. Look at Jenny's vacation pictures. What do you think she says about her trip?

B. 🎧 **MODEL CONVERSATION.** Listen and practice.

PICTURE #1

Ann: Hey Jenny, how was your trip?

Jenny: It was great. New Zealand was fantastic. Look, I just got the pictures.

Ann: Wow, look at this one. ==What's with the dressy clothes?== You're wearing a dress!

Jenny: We're celebrating my friend Jackie's birthday. We went to her favorite Italian restaurant.

Ann: Very stylish. Who are these guys?

Jenny: The one in the white shirt is Thomas. He's Jackie's brother. And that's Eric, in the blue shirt. He's a friend.

Ann: I want to go to New Zealand . . .

IDIOM

What's with the dressy clothes? = Why are you wearing dressy clothes?

C. 🎧 **ACTIVE LISTENING.** Listen and check (✓) the answers.

PICTURE #2

1. What are they playing?
   ☐ volleyball   ☐ rugby   ☐ soccer
2. Is Jenny playing?
   ☐ Yes   ☐ No
3. How long did they play?
   ☐ two hours   ☐ all day
   ☐ all morning   ☐ three hours

PICTURE #3

1. What time of year is it?
   ☐ summer   ☐ spring   ☐ winter
2. Whose coat is Jenny wearing?
   ☐ Jackie's   ☐ her own   ☐ Eric's
3. What did they do?
   ☐ went skiing   ☐ went sightseeing
   ☐ went hiking   ☐ went shopping

A. 🎧 **PRONUNCIATION.** Listen and practice the questions and answers.

QUESTIONS				ANSWERS	
What	are	you they	doing?	I'm They're	listening to music. running.
	is	she	wearing?	She's	wearing jeans.

More Pronunciation Practice

Reduced forms of "what are" and "what is he" Turn to page 93.

B. GET IT RIGHT. Describe the people in the pictures. What are they doing? What are they wearing? Use verbs from the box.

Verbs

listen to music	talk	run*
drink coffee	sing	play the piano

1. They are running. They're wearing shorts, T-shirts and athletic shoes.

3. _____

2. _____

4. _____

C. YOUR IDEAS. Ask your partner what people in your class are wearing and doing. Use the Idea box and your own ideas.

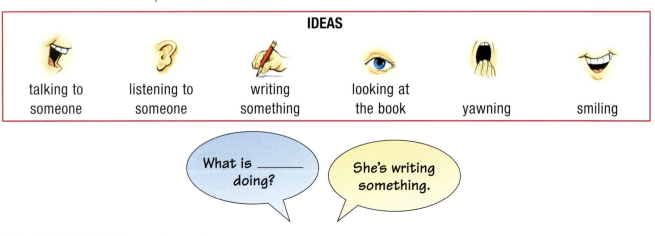

IDEAS

talking to someone   listening to someone   writing something   looking at the book   yawning   smiling

What is _____ doing?

She's writing something.

4 CONVERSATION STRATEGY: *Showing surprise*

A. 🎧 **PRONUNCIATION.** Listen and practice the expressions.

> Really!

> You're kidding!

> You're not serious!

B. 🎧 **LISTEN and ADD.** Write the missing expressions. Then practice with a partner.

1. A: What do you think of nose rings?

B: I like them.

A: _____!

B: No, I really like them. I think they're cool.

2. A: That's a nice jacket.

B: Thanks. I bought it five years ago.

A: _____!

B: Yeah, and it's still in style.

5 TALKATHON: *Clothing questionnaire*

A. DISCUSS and DECIDE. Work with a partner. Add three questions about clothes to the list below.

Questions	_____'s answers	_____'s answers
1. What do you hate to wear?		
2. Where do you shop for clothes?		
3. Are you wearing your favorite color today?		
4.		
5.		
6.		

B. TALK AROUND. Interview two classmates. Write their answers in the chart. Remember to show suprise at an unexpected answer.

C. REPORT. Tell the most surprising thing about your classmates.

School Uniforms

What did you wear to school? What did you think of your school clothes?

◄ Senri Middle School

Yoko: We hated our school uniforms. They were too dressy. The ties were uncomfortable. The dresses were comfortable but ugly. We wanted to wear pants to school, especially in the winter.

► Highland Elementary School

Heather: We liked our school uniforms. They were very casual, and we had a lot of choice. In the picture, some kids are wearing khaki shorts, skirts, and pants. Some kids are wearing green shirts and some are wearing white shirts. We didn't have any special shoes to wear. Our only problem was that there weren't any shorts for the girls.

▼ Staples High School

Dylan: We were very lucky. We didn't have school uniforms. In the picture, we're all wearing jeans and casual shirts or sweaters. That's what most students usually wore. No one wore dressy clothes to school.

▲ San Marcos High School

Carlos: As you can see, we wore a school uniform. Boys and girls both wore yellow shirts, but we could wear different color shorts, pants or skirts. Students usually wore athletic shoes. Our school uniforms were pretty comfortable.

READ ABOUT IT

A. Complete the sentences.

1. Yoko, Heather and Carlos wore a _____ to school, but Dylan didn't.

2. The students at Senri Middle School _____ their uniforms.

3. Girls can wear _____ at San Marcos High School but not at Highland Elementary School.

4. Students at Highland Elementary School and San Marcos High School sometimes wore _____ shoes.

B. Read your sentences to a partner.

TALK ABOUT IT

Take turns asking and answering questions.

1. Which uniform do you prefer? Why?

2. Did you wear a uniform to school? If yes, describe it. Did you like it? Why or why not?

3. Do you think school uniforms are a good idea? Why or why not?

4. Your question: _____?

WRITE ABOUT IT

A. Make notes about the clothes you wore to school and your opinions about them.

Clothes you wore to school	Your opinions
1.	1.
2.	2.
3.	3.
4.	4.

B. Write about the clothes you and your friends wore to school and your opinions of them.

EXAMPLE:

> My school didn't have school uniforms. We wore lots of different things. Sometimes we wore jeans and T-shirts or sweaters. I often liked to wear skirts and dresses, but my friends didn't. They usually wore pants. I think it was good to have a choice. Each person looked different. I liked that.

Project Idea
Gallery Walk:
Future uniforms
Design a school uniform for the year 2040 and write a description of the design. Display the designs and have a "gallery walk" to look at them.

Review of Units 10-12

1 CONVERSATION

A. Complete the conversation.

A: Hi, Mark. It's Annie. What are you _____?

B: Oh, I'm _____ TV. How about you?

A: _____ shopping downtown. I want _____ buy a shirt for my brother. Where's a good place to _____ men's clothes?

B: _____ you try Edgar's Fine Clothing?

A: Excuse _____?

B: Edgar's Fine Clothing.

A: Edgar's? _____ that?

B: It's next to Bob's Books.

A: Great. Thanks.

B. 🎧 Listen to check your answers. Then practice with a partner.

2 INFORMATION GAP

Student A, look at the information below. Student B, turn to page 85.

STUDENT A

A. Read about Keiko and answer your partner's questions.

Keiko
I have to wear dressy clothes a lot because of my work. I wear a skirt and jacket to work every day. I need to buy more casual clothes for weekends. Once in a while I wear casual clothes to work. On special occasions I usually wear a dress and high heels. In the summer I wear shorts once in a while.

B. Ask your partner questions about Tom.

1. Does Tom like to wear casual clothes? Why?
2. How often does Tom wear sweatshirts?
3. When does Tom wear his fleece jacket and boots?
4. How often does Tom wear a suit and tie?
5. What does Tom wear in the summer?

A. Look at the picture for two minutes. What are the people wearing? What are they doing?

B. 🎧 Cover the picture. Listen to the questions and write your answers.

1. _____	5. _____
2. _____	6. _____
3. _____	7. _____
4. _____	8. _____

Review of Units 1-3: Information Gap for Student B

STUDENT B: Interview your partner and complete the chart.

> A: Where's a good place to visit?
>
> B: _____

> A: What sports . . .?
>
> B: _____

	Good place to visit "Where's a good . . ."	Popular sports "What sports…"	Popular foods "What kind of food…"	Weather "How's…"	Shopping "How's…"	Nightlife "How's…"
Student A	_____					
Student B	Hawaii			☺	☹	😐

Review of Units 4-6: Information Gap for Student B

STUDENT B

A. Answer your partner's questions about the activities in the chart below. Then ask your partner about each activity. Write *Yes* or *No* in the chart. Answer your partner's questions.

A: Do you <u>like to listen to rap music?</u>   B: <u>Yes, I do. I think it's great.</u>

	like to listen to rap music?	like to watch horror movies?	like to go dancing?	like to play volleyball?	want to eat out tonight?
Do you . . .	_____	_____	_____	_____	_____
Does David . . .	_____	Yes	_____	_____	No
Does Nina . . .	No	_____	Yes	Yes	_____

Review of Units 4-6: Information Gap for Student B (Cont.)

2. Take turns asking questions about David and Nina. Write *Yes* or *No* in the chart.

A: Does David <u>like to listen to rap music</u>?   B: <u>Yes, he does.</u>

3. Write four sentences about the people in the chart.

Both David and Nina _____ .

David _____ , but Nina doesn't.

My partner and Nina _____ .

My partner and David _____ .

Review of Units 10-12: Information Gap for Student B

STUDENT B

A. Ask your partner questions about Keiko.

1. How often does Keiko wear a skirt and jacket to work?
2. What does Keiko need to buy? Why?
3. How often does Keiko wear casual clothes to work?
4. What does Keiko wear on special occasions?
5. When does Keiko wear shorts?

B. Read about Tom. Then answer your partner's questions.

Tom

I love my casual clothes because they are comfortable. I wear sweatshirts a lot. I wear my fleece jacket and boots all the time in the winter. I never wear a shirt and tie to classes. Once in a while I wear a suit and tie for a job interview. In the summer I wear shorts and sandals a lot.

Pronunciation

UNIT 1 Intonation of *yes/no* questions

A. 🎧 Listen to these questions. Note the rising intonation.

Is fondue Swiss?

Is fondue spicy?

Are bananas good?

Are bananas cheap?

Is French food delicious?

Is French food expensive?

Are hamburgers American?

Are hamburgers good for you?

B. 🎧 Listen and practice the questions above.

C. 🎧 Listen and practice the conversation with a partner. Notice the intonation of *yes/no* questions.

A: Is tofu good?

B: I don't know.

A: Is kim chee spicy?

B: I'm not sure.

A: Are tacos cheap?

B: Beats me.

A: Are you tired of my questions?

B: Yes, I am. Please be quiet.

UNIT 2 Intonation of *wh-* questions

A. 🎧 Listen to these questions. Notice the rising and falling intonation.

What's your favorite sport?

What's your favorite kind of food?

Where is volleyball popular?

Where is sushi popular?

Why is volleyball exciting?

B. 🎧 Listen and practice the questions above.

C. 🎧 Listen to the conversation. Then practice with a partner.

A: What's your favorite sport?

B: My favorite sport is running.

A: Running? How come?

B: It's healthy and it's fun.

A: Where do you run?

B: In the park.

A: When do you run?

B: Not after dark!

UNIT 3 Syllable Stress in adjectives

A. 🎧 Listen to the examples. Notice the stressed syllable.

•	•	•	•
awful	interesting	terrific	international

B. 🎧 Listen and practice the words above.

C. 🎧 Listen to the adjectives and mark the stressed syllable.

1. wonderful   **4.** horrible

2. funny   **5.** expensive

3. delicious   **6.** relaxing

D. 🎧 Listen to the conversations. Then practice them with a partner.

1. A: How is the food at this restaurant?
   B: It's wonderful!
   A: Is it expensive?
   B: A little.

2. A: How's the traffic this morning?
   B: It's terrible.
   A: How's the weather?
   B: It's awful.

3. A: How's the hotel?
   B: It's beautiful. It's very international.
   A: How's the beach?
   B: Relaxing.

4. A: How's the book?
   B: It's interesting.
   A: Is it funny?
   B: No, it's sad.

UNIT 4 Reduced form of *do you*

A. 🎧 Listen to these questions. Notice two ways to say *Do you*.

Do you like jazz?   Do you like golf?
Do you like pizza?   Do you like New York?

B. 🎧 Listen and repeat the chant. Then practice it in pairs and groups.

A: Do you like hip hop?

B: *No. Do you?*

A: Yes, I do. Do you like jazz?

B: *No. Do you?*

A: Yes, I do. Do you like salsa?

B: *No. Do you?*

A: Yes, I do. Do you like rock?

B: *No. Do you?*

A: Yes, I do. Do you like me?

B: *Do I like you? Yes I do.*

C. Ask your partner these questions. Use the reduced form of *do you*.

1. Do you have any pets?   **3.** Do you like extreme sports?

2. Do you travel a lot?   **4.** Do you like to cook?

UNIT 5 Word stress in sentences

A. 🎧 Listen to the conversation. Notice the word stress.

A: Do you like **movies**?

B: No, I **love** movies.

A: What **kind** of movies do you like?

B: I like **horror** movies.

A: **Horror** movies? Really? I **hate** horror movies!

B: So, what kind of movies do **you** like?

A: I like **comedies.**

B: Really? I **hate** comedies.

A: No way! **Everybody** likes comedies!

B. Practice the conversation above with a partner.

C. 🎧 Listen and <u>underline</u> the stressed words. The first one is done for you.

1. I don't like <u>action</u> movies. I like <u>comedies</u>.

2. My best friend likes musicals. What about your best friend?

3. Everybody likes animated movies.

4. Young people love it.

5. I like science fiction movies. She likes romances.

6. I love horror movies. I hate comedies.

D. Practice the sentences in Activity C above.

UNIT 6 Reduced form of *want to*

A. 🎧 Listen to these conversations. Notice two ways to say *want to*.

1. **A:** What do you want to do?
   B: I want to watch a video

2. **A:** Do you want to go out?
   B: No, I want to stay home.

B. 🎧 Listen and repeat the chant. Then practice it in groups and pairs.

A: What do you want to do? Do you want to eat pizza?

B: *I don't know.*

A: What do you want to do? Do you want to watch a movie?

B: *I don't know.*

A: What do you want to do? Do you want to go dancing?

B: *I don't know.*

A: What do you want to do? Do you want to do ANYTHING?

B: *Of course! I want to stay home with you!*

C. Tell your partner three things you want to do after class today and three things you want to do next year.

UNIT 7 Reduced form of *wh-* questions

A. 🎧 Listen to the questions. Notice two ways to say *what do you* and *when do you*.

1. What do you do for fun?
2. What do you do in the morning?
3. What do you do in the evening?

4. When do you eat breakfast?
5. When do you study English?
6. When do you watch TV?

B. 🎧 Listen and practice the questions above.

C. Add two more questions of your own. Then ask and answer the questions above with a partner.

UNIT 8 Sentence stress—content words

A. 🎧 Listen to the sentences. Notice that the last word or word group in each sentence is stressed.

1. I live on instant noodles and **diet soda**.
2. Running is easy for **Anna**.
3. George is very **tired**.

4. How often do you get enough **sleep**?
5. How often do you **exercise**?
6. How much time do you spend with **friends**?

B. 🎧 Listen to these sentences and underline the stressed word or word group. You will hear each sentence twice.

1. I go to the gym a lot.
2. Do you watch a lot of TV?
3. Meditation can add years to your life.
4. What do you do to relax?
5. I eat a lot of junk food.
6. I do a lot of things that make me laugh.

C. 🎧 Listen again and practice the sentences above.

UNIT 9 -ed endings

A. 🎧 Listen to the examples. Listen again and repeat them.

walked /t/　　　dreamed /d/　　　started /ed/

B. 🎧 Do you hear /t/, /d/, or /ed/? Listen and check [✓].

	/t/	/d/	/ed/
1. listened			
2. stopped			
3. watched			
4. needed			
5. played			
6. checked			
7. exercised			
8. wanted			

C. Practice the conversations below with a partner.

1. A: Did you drive here?
B: No, I walked.

2. A: What time did you start?
B: I started at about 3:00.

3. A: What did you do last night?
B: Oh, I just listened to music.

4. A: Why did you go to the store?
B: I needed some bread.

5. A: What did you do last night?
B: Nothing special. I watched a boring movie on TV.

6. A: Did you have fun yesterday?
B: Yes! I played baseball with my friends.

UNIT 10 Initial *th* sounds

A. 🎧 There are two ways to pronounce *th* in English: /th/ as in *there* and /th/ as in *think*. Which sound do you hear? Listen and check [✓].

	/th/ as in *there*	/th/ as in *think*
1. thin		
2. they		
3. then		
4. thing		
5. this		
6. that		
7. three		
8. the		

B. 🎧 Listen and practice these sentences.

1. He is very thin.

2. They have three cats.

3. What did you do then?

4. There are many good things about my neighborhood.

5. This is my favorite store.

6. I think the store opens at nine-thirty.

C. Tongue twister. Say the following sentence three times quickly:

They think there are three thin cats in that thing over there.

A. 🎧 Listen. Do you hear /s/, /z/ or /ez/? Check [✓].

	/s/	**/z/**	**/ez/**
1. supplies			
2. cosmetics			
3. gifts			
4. clothes			
5. DVDs			
6. dresses			
7. books			
8. shoes			
9. purchases			
10. places			

B. 🎧 Listen again and repeat the words in the chart.

C. Tell your partner five things that you want to buy. Choose from the box.

| CDs   cosmetics   magazines   shoes |
| pants   glasses   used books |
| suitcases   clothes |
| pens   notebooks   cars   gifts |

UNIT 12 Reduced forms of *what are* and *what is he*

A. 🎧 Listen and repeat the chants. Notice the pronunciation of *what are* and *what is he*.

Chant 1

A: What are you wearing today?

B: Jeans.

A: What are you learning at school?

B: Math.

A: What are you eating for lunch?

B: Soup.

A: What are you doing right now?

B: Nothing!

Chant 2

A: What is he wearing today?

B: Jeans.

A: What is he learning at school?

B: Math.

A: What is he eating for lunch?

B: Soup.

A: What is he doing right now?

B: Nothing!

B. Practice the chant in pairs and groups.

C. Ask and answer the questions from the chant with a partner. Give your own answers. For the second part, ask about another student in your class.

Vocabulary Summary

Nouns: *Food*
bananas
bread
cookies
crepes
feijoada
fondue
hamburgers
spaghetti
sushi

Other nouns
dish
food
restaurant
words

Pronouns
I
it
me
you

Possessives
my
your

Other new words I learned

_____

_____

Adjectives: *Nationalities*
Argentinean
Australian
Brazilian
Canadian
Chinese
French
Indian
Italian
Japanese
Korean
Filipino
Swiss
Thai
Vietnamese

Other adjectives
cheap
delicious
expensive
favorite
good
spicy

Verbs
are/is/am
eat
know
like

_____

_____

Question words
how
what

Prepositions
about
in

Other
let's
not
partner
sure
that
too
well
yes

_____

_____

Nouns: *Sports*
auto racing
baseball
basketball
golf
gymnastics
ice hockey
rugby
running
skiing
snowboarding
soccer
surfing
swimming
taekwondo
tennis
volleyball

Other nouns
team
school
friends

Other new words I learned

_____

_____

Adjectives
boring
dangerous
difficult
easy
exciting
expensive
fun
global
great
popular
relaxing

Verbs
play
think
isn't

_____

_____

Prepositions
at

Other
because
everywhere
our
really
where

_____

_____

UNIT 3

Nouns
beach
bird
horseback riding
nightlife
place
shopping
traffic
transportation
vacation
weather

Adjectives
awful
bad
fantastic
fine
horrible
interesting
ok
public
wonderful

Expressions
Wow!
Yeah!

Other
for
hello
here
hi
oh
there
they're

Other new words I learned
_____   _____
_____   _____
_____   _____

UNIT 4

Nouns: *Kinds of music*
bluegrass
classical music
country music
jazz
opera
rap
reggae
rock
rhythm and blues
samba

Other nouns
beat
brother
girlfriend
music
parents
teacher

Adjectives
cool
different
terrific

Verbs
does
doesn't
dance
has
love

Pronouns
he
she
we

Other
very

Other new words I learned
_____   _____
_____   _____
_____   _____

UNIT 5

Nouns: *Kinds of movies*
action movie
animated movie
comedy
drama
horror movie
musical
science fiction movie

Other nouns
child
class
customer
man
people
person
woman

Pronouns
both
everybody
few
some

Verbs
can
hate
help
need
let
recommend
see
want
welcome

Other
thanks
who

Other new words I learned

_____ _____
_____ _____
_____ _____

UNIT 6

Nouns
afternoon
concert
dancing
event
group
home
night
noodle
party
pizza
sister
take-out
food
video
wrestling

Adjectives
broke
busy
crowded
smoky

Verbs
can't
chat
go
hang out
invite
prefer
stay
try
watch

Prepositions
on
out
to
with

Time words
tonight
weekend

Other
always
hey
I'd
online
something
sorry

Other new words I learned

_____ _____
_____ _____
_____ _____

UNIT 7

Nouns
bed
co-workers
days
dinner
e-mail
hours
information
job
lunch
mall
newspaper
travel
agency

Prepositions
after
around

Adjectives
big
common
early
late

Verbs
begin
check
close
get
have
help
leave
open
study
show

Time Words
evening
midnight
morning
weekdays
6:00 A.M.
12:15 P.M.

Other
more
part-time
straight
up
usually

Other new words I learned

_____   _____
_____   _____
_____   _____

UNIT 8

Nouns
diet soda
doctor
exam
gym
health
junk food
marathon
stuff
vegetables
vitamins

Adjectives
healthy
impressive
instant
tired

Verbs
drink
exercise
feel
look
run
sleep
smoke
spend
take

Frequency Words
every day
four times a week
how often
never
once a week
twice a year

Other
enough
outdoors
today

Other new words I learned

_____   _____
_____   _____
_____   _____

UNIT 9

Nouns
best friend games
coffee laundry
computer nap
family

Adjectives
new
nice
special
right

Verbs
eat/ate
go/went
meet/met
play/played
stay/stayed
take/took
talk/talked
walk/walked

Other
actually
anyone
else
later
nothing
someone

Other new words I learned

_____   _____
_____   _____
_____   _____

UNIT 10

Nouns: *Places*
art museum
bank
bookstore
CD store
coffee shop
convenience store
department store
downtown
drugstore
gas station
movie theatre
newsstand
shopping mall
subway station

Other nouns
ATM (automated teller
  machine)
area
bus
directions
mailbox
neighborhood
problem
taxi
visitor

Prepositions
across
between
near
next to

Other
any

Other new words I learned

_____   _____
_____   _____
_____   _____

UNIT 11

Nouns
ball
book
clothes
clothing
cosmetics
DVDs
electronic equipment
gifts
house
jewelry
magazine
money
month
necklace
newspaper
notebook
occasion
office
paper
pen
pencil
reading material
ring
(school) supplies
suggestions
T-shirt

Adjectives
last
near
recent

Verbs
buy
spend

Other
how much
together
yesterday

Other new words I learned
_____ _____
_____ _____
_____ _____

UNIT 12

Nouns: *Clothes*
athletic shoes   sandals
blouse   shorts
casual pants   shirt
dress   skirt
fleece jacket   suit
high heels   sweater
hiking boots   sweatshirt
jeans   tie
nose ring

Adjectives
cool
dressy
fantastic
stylish
uncomfortable

Other nouns
birthday   trip
piano   wedding
spring   winter
summer

Verbs
celebrating   smiling
doing   talking to
listening   wearing
looking at   writing
sightseeing   yawning

Other
while

Other new words I learned
_____ _____
_____ _____
_____ _____

Irregular Simple Past Verbs

Present	Simple Past	Present	Simple Past
be	was/were	lend	lent
become	became	lose	lost
begin	began	make	made
break	broke	meet	met
bring	brought	pay	paid
buy	bought	put	put
catch	caught	read	read
choose	chose	ride	rode
come	came	run	ran
cost	cost	say	said
do	did	see	saw
draw	drew	sell	sold
drink	drank	send	sent
drive	drove	shut	shut
eat	ate	sing	sang
fall	fell	sleep	slept
feel	felt	speak	spoke
fight	fought	spend	spent
find	found	stand	stood
fly	flew	steal	stole
forget	forgot	swim	swam
get	got	take	took
give	gave	teach	taught
go	went	tell	told
grow	grew	think	thought
have	had	throw	threw
hear	heard	understand	understood
hit	hit	wake	woke
keep	kept	wear	wore
know	knew	win	won
leave	left	write	wrote

Credits

ILLUSTRATIONS

Reggie Holladay 16, 18, 19, 22, 24, 36, 37, 39, 43, 44, 47, 48, 63, 77, 78, 84
Jonathan Massie 43, 63, 66, 83
Bill Petersen 5, 6, 7, 8, 10, 13, 50, 56, 59, 65

PHOTOGRAPHICS CREDITS

2 (*top*) © Real Life Images/Stock Connection/PictureQuest; (*bottom, left to right*) © PhotoDisc/Getty Images; © MTPA Stock/Masterfile

3 © Digital Vision/Getty Images

4 (*top, left to right*) © Joe Pellegrini/FoodPix/Getty Images; © Nik Wheeler/CORBIS; © James Baigrie/FoodPix/Getty Images; (*bottom, left to right*) © PhotoDisc/Getty Images; © Eric Futran/FoodPix/Getty Images; © Christel Rosenfeld/Stone/Getty Images

8 (*top, left to right*) © Felicia Martinez/PhotoEdit; © Sally Ullman/FoodPix/Getty Images; (*middle, left to right*) © FoodPix/Getty Images; © PhotoDisc Red/Getty Images; (*bottom, left to right*) © Tony Freeman/PhotoEdit; © Janet Bailey/Masterfile

11 (*left to right*) © Thinkstock/PictureQuest; © Photo Researchers, Inc.; © Thinkstock/Getty Images; ©ThinkStock/SuperStock; © Allsport Concepts/Getty Images

12 AP/Wide World Photos

14 (*closewise, from top left*) © Duomo/CORBIS; © Michael Newman/PhotoEdit; © AFP/CORBIS; © VISUM/The Image Works

17 Jack Demuth

19 © Lake County Museum/CORBIS

20 (*closewise, from top left*) © Stephen Saks/IndexStock; © Gary Braasch/CORBIS; © P. Scholey/SuperStock; © Yoshio Tomii/SuperStock; © Dave G. Houser/CORBIS

22 © Royalty-Free/CORBIS

25 (*left, top to bottom*) © Bill Bachman/The Image Works; © Tim Kiusalaas/Masterfile; © Stuart McClymont/Getty Images; (*right*) AP/Wide World Photos

26 © Martin Meyer/Zefa Collection/Masterfile

27 (*left to right*) © Reuters NewMedia Inc./CORBIS; © AFP/CORBIS

28 (*closewise, from top left*) © Robert Fried; © Lawrence Manning/CORBIS; ©ThinkStock/SuperStock; © Allen Birnbach/Masterfile; © Dave Bartruff/IndexStock

30 (*top, left to right*) © SuperStock; © Dreamworks/courtesy Everett Collection; © SuperStock; © Douglas Kirkland/CORBIS (bottom, left to right) S.S. Archives/Shooting Star; Warner Brothers/Shooting Star; © Buena Vista Pictures/courtesy Everett Collection; © Dreamworks/courtesy Everett Collection

31 Jack Demuth

32 © Powerstock/SuperStock

33 Photofest

34 (*top, left to right*) 20th Century Fox/Shooting Star; Photofest; (*bottom, left to right*) Photofest; © Warner Brothers/courtesy Everett

37 Jack Demuth

39 © Anthony Redpath/CORBIS

40 (*closewise, from top left*) © Kenneth Hamm/Photo Japan; © Larry Luxner; © Oscar C. Williams; © Dinodia Picture Agency

42 (*top*) © Peter Barrett/Masterfile; (*bottom*) © ElektraVision/Wonderfile

45 (*left to right*) © Michelle Bridwell/PhotoEdit; © Margot Grantses/The Image Works; © David Hanover/CORBIS

46 © David Young-Wolff/PhotoEdit

48 (*closewise, from top left*) © Reuters NewMedia Inc./CORBIS; Photofest; © Lisette Le Bon/SuperStock; Photo by Paul Morales

51 Jack Demuth

52 © Chuck Mason/ImageState

53 © Digital Visions/Getty Images

54 (*closewise, from top*) © Pixland.com/Wonderfile; © Syracuse Newspapers/The Image Works; © Rob Lewine/CORBIS; © Masterfile

57 Jack Demuth

60 (*closewise, from top left*) ©LWA-Dann Tardif/CORBIS; © David Young Wolff/PhotoEdit; © LWA-Sharie Kennedy/CORBIS; © John Henley/CORBIS

62 © Jon Feingersh/Masterfile

64 (*top, left to right*) © Sonda Dawes/The Image Works; © Jeremy Horner/CORBIS; © Ron Sherman/Stone/Getty Images; © Gail Mooney/CORBIS; (*bottom, left to right*) © Bill Aron/Photo Edit; © Paul Kenward/Stone/Getty Images; © Tim Page/CORBIS; © Hackenberg/Zefa/Masterfile

67 Michael Newman/PhotoEdit

68 (*closewise, from top left*) © Andy Sacks/Stone/Getty Images; © Jurgen Reisch/Taxi/Getty Images; © West Rock/Taxi/Getty Images; © Paul Barton/CORBIS

Credits (Continued)

71 *(top, left to right)* © PhotoDisc/Getty Images; Courtesy of KNTO *(Korea National Tourism Organization)*; *(bottom)* © Jiang Jin/SuperStock

72 © Chuck Savage/CORBIS

73 © Anton Vengo/SuperStock

74 *(top)* © Nacy Richmond/The Image Works; *(bottom)* © Ed Bock/CORBIS

79 ©Don Marr/SuperStock

80 *(closewise, from top left)* © Deborah Davis/Photo Edit; AP/Wide World Photos; © Barbara Stitzer/PhotoEdit;

© Jacques Langevin/CORBIS SYGMA

82 *(top, left to right)* © George Shelley/Masterfile; © Jose Luis Pelaez, Inc./CORBIS; *(middle)* © Royalty-Free/CORBIS; *(bottom)* © Sonda Dawes/The Image Works

84 *(top)* © Peter Barrett/Masterfile; *(bottom)* © ElektraVision/Wonderfile

85 *(top)* © Royalty-Free/CORBIS; *(bottom)* © Sonda Dawes/The Image Works